THE FRONT FOUR

Books
by
Howard Liss

The Front Four
AFL Dream Backfield
The Making of a Rookie
Father & Son Baseball Book
Football Talk for Beginners
Basketball Talk for Beginners
Triple-Crown Winners
Soccer, the International Game
Lacrosse
Goal!
Unidentified Flying Objects
The Mighty Mekong
Asgeir of Iceland
Yogi Berra's Baseball Guidebook
Adolph Rupp's Basketball Guidebook

let's meet at the quarterback

the front 4

by Howard Liss

a Lion Book

Copyright © 1971 by Howard Liss
Published by Lion Books
52 Park Avenue, New York, N.Y. 10016
All rights reserved
Published simultaneously in Canada by George J. McLeod Ltd., 73 Bathurst Street, Toronto 2B, Ontario
ISBN: 0-87460-238-6
Library edition: 0-87460-260-2
Library of Congress Catalog Card Number: 75-127396
Manufactured in the United States of America.

CONTENTS

Acknowledgments	vii
How the Front Fours Began	9
Landry's Legions	22
Lombardi's Blocks of Granite	34
A Pride of Lions	46
The Doomsday Defense	61
The Fearsome Foursome	75
Braase, Miller, and Two Guys Named Smith	89
The Purple People Eaters	105
The No-Nickname Line	120
Appendix: Official Play-by-play of Detroit Lions vs. Green Bay Packers, November 22, 1962	135

ACKNOWLEDGMENTS

The author wishes to express his deepest gratitude to Pete Rozelle, Commissioner of Professional Football; to his able staff, especially Joe Browne, Don Weiss, Jim Kensil, and Harold Rosenthal; and to the attractive secretaries and efficient keepers of the files, all of whom cheerfully gave of their time and counsel.

How the Front Fours Began

SEVERAL YEARS AGO A NATIONAL MAGAZINE published a full-page photograph of a football player who had just been zapped. The man was Y. A. Tittle, one of the greatest passers in the history of the game. Old Yat was sitting on his haunches, blood streaming from a cut on his face, his unseeing, unfocused eyes staring across the field. A defensive lineman had caught him from the blind side and creamed him. Tittle had been hit so hard that his helmet cracked!

After his scrambled senses had been somewhat restored, Tittle admitted that the lineman had done nothing illegal. The defensive specialist had merely obeyed the first rule of defensive line play: *Get the Quarterback!* Belt him! Batter him! Blast him! In that respect football—especially professional style—had returned to the savagery of the turn of the century, when the game was so violent that President Theodore Roosevelt insisted that the rules be amended before entire teams were destroyed.

The two types of players involved in the Tittle incident—the dandy passer and the hulking defensive linemen—were comparatively new to the game. In fact, before World War II there was very little difference between offensive and defensive football players, because—they were the same players. At that time two-platoon football was not yet widespread. Most of the personnel were "60-minute men," including the running backs and the quarterback.

For example, in the 1934 National Football League championship game between the Chicago Bears and the New York Giants, New York used only four substitutes. Cecil Irvin and Bill Morgan, the tackles; Ed Danowski at quarterback, and Ken Strong at halfback were rested part of the time. The Bears used only seven subs.

In the 1937 championship game between the Bears and the Washington Redskins, Sammy Baugh—one of the deadliest of the early passers—played a whale of a game on defense, making one of the key tackles that shut off the potential tying touchdown. Today, a pro football coach would be taken to a mental hospital in a straitjacket if he so much as contemplated throwing his star passer into the defensive backfield.

Yet, while professional football players of that era were rugged men, they weren't particularly tall or heavy. Very few went over the 225-pound mark, including the linemen. A quarterback might weigh in at 170—and often less. The running backs averaged 185 to 200 pounds at the most. The immortal Bronco Nagurski of the Chicago Bears played fullback on offense and tackle on defense. By today's standards, a fullback must weigh *at least* 220 pounds, and the defensive tackle about 250. Yet Nagurski averaged 190 pounds over the course of a season. And nobody ever ran harder or tackled more viciously than that wild horse from northern Minnesota.

Probably those hardy souls could last out an hour or slightly less of a hard game because football was much simpler in the prewar days. The offense was built around the single-wing or double-wing formations. The single wing generated good running power because the tailback had three backfield blockers in front of him to serve as ready-made interference on end sweeps or power plays into the line. The double wing was ideally suited to deception, with deep reverses, end-around plays, fakes, and tricky jump passes. But in either case the attack was relatively simple by modern standards. The defense could set itself. There were few surprises.

By the same token the offense could read the defense very well. Most of the time the opposition used the all-purpose 6–2–2–1 formation. There were six evenly spaced linemen at the line of scrimmage; a couple of yards behind, lending support to the tackles, were two linebackers; two wingmen were spread toward the sidelines, approximately where today's corner halfbacks are stationed; and the single safety stood like a lone eagle somewhat farther back, about twenty yards or so behind the line, in the center of the formation.

This defensive alignment could be varied somewhat, especially against a team with a strong running attack. Against such opponents the 7–2–2 proved useful, or it could be shifted into a 7–1–2–1, sometimes called the "7-diamond defense." When a team found itself pushed back into the shadow of its own goal posts, the defense would form into an eight-man line with three linebackers. But basically that was about as much as the alignment could be altered, and further variations weren't necessary.

Late in the 1930's a couple of Illinois football coaches put their heads together and began to tinker with the established traditions of the game. One of them was Clark Shaughnessy, head coach of the woefully inept University of Chicago team. The other was George "Papa Bear" Halas, owner-coach of the Chicago Bears. They talked about the strategy of football, and they drew thousands of diagrams, and they experimented.

The result of all that burned midnight oil was the T formation.

There was nothing basically new about the formation itself. In fact it was probably the oldest form of offense in football, with the single and double wings coming in much later. However, the old T had never been properly exploited, and gradually the game had changed so much, with new rules and regulations, that it was almost forgotten. By returning to a variation of the T, Halas and Shaughnessy changed the entire philosophy of football. And the evolutionary changes are still going on.

In the single and double wings, the tailback was positioned about five yards behind the center. The quarterback barked signals from his spot behind guard. The center snapped the ball back between his legs to the tailback, who could run with the ball or give it to someone else, or pass it (the quarterback was by no means the only passer on the team in those days). A player like Sammy Baugh, or some other good passer, often filled the tailback slot. Baugh wasn't a bad runner, but he passed more often than he carried the ball.

Halas and Shaughnessy began their alterations by moving the quarterback directly behind the center. The ball was no longer snapped back; rather it was a kind of exchange, with the center handing the ball back through his legs. The two halfbacks and the fullback were about five yards behind the center-quarterback duo to form the *basic T formation*.

Even as the first practice plays were being run off, it was evident that the new offense had several built-in advantages. Because the quarterback got his hands on the ball quicker, plays erupted faster. The game was speeded up noticeably. The running attack improved. When the quarterback got the ball, the running backs were permitted to start moving forward. A ball carrier was under a full head of steam as he took the handoff from the quarterback, and thus he had more power in his "dive plays."

In a kind of chain reaction, the improved forward rush of

the ball carrier made life easier for the offensive line. Before, a guard or tackle had to hold a block on his opponent for several seconds, until the running back reached the hole he had created. Now, with proper timing, the offensive lineman merely had to "brush block" his opponent; that is, shove him hard, create the momentary opening through which the running back could wriggle, then release the block, for by that time the ball carrier was through the hole. Those dive plays were often good for a couple of yards at a crack, which made them an excellent call on third-and-two situations. The "quick opener," as it came to be called, soon was a bread-and-butter play for every T formation team.

The deception possibilities of the T were almost endless. The quarterback could fake or hand off to three different potential ball carriers, all stationed behind him. But one thing he could *not* do very well was run with the ball himself. Except for the linemen in front, he had no other interference. However, he could always fake a handoff, drop back, and throw the ball. Thus the quarterback stopped running with the football (except on keeper plays requiring a yard or two for a first down or touchdown). He handed off or he threw the ball. Nothing else. No blocking, no line plays, and only an occasional keeper or bootleg play.

As Shaughnessy and Halas continued to experiment, they also began to realize that everything in the new offense hinged on one key man—the quarterback. Not only did he have to know when to call a particular play, and handle the ball well, but also, he became the team's primary passer. The job wasn't that easy, either. Counting fakes and variations of plays, the Chicago Bears' playbook contained approximately 400 plays. Any number of them started out the same way and ended differently. For example, the quarterback could fake to the fullback, turn, and hand off to the halfback. Or he could hand off to the fullback, turn, and fake a handoff to the halfback. Or he could fake to both, drop back, and pass. So, where was Halas going to find a man with the brains of a Phi Beta Kappa and the passing ability of a Sammy Baugh?

Fortunately, such a man was available in the person of Sid Luckman, the magnificent quarterback from Columbia University. Luckman had been trained in the single-wing attack during his college career, but every other quarterback was a single-wing or double-wing signal caller in those days. Columbia Sid had the sharpness to adapt quickly to the T. He had already proved conclusively that he could throw the ball as well as any other college passer, and better than most.

Of course the good running backs were needed too, and Halas either had them or got them. They included such stars as George McAfee, Bill Osmanski, and Ray Nolting, powerhouses one and all. To catch Luckman's passes, Halas employed Kenny Kavanaugh, rated as one of the dozen top receivers of all time.

It took a while to get the attack squared away. In 1940, when Luckman and the Bears put it all together, Chicago's "Monsters of the Midway" lost a couple of games during the regular season, including one to Washington. But in the championship playoff game against Sammy Baugh and the Redskins, Chicago's attack suddenly jelled into a thundering tornado as the Bears stomped the opposition into the dirt by a score of 73–0! That game, more than anything else that happened before or afterward, sounded the death knell for single-wing football, at least in the pro game.

There are those who maintain that football strategy and battlefield strategy are really the same thing. It all boils down to adjustment. The offense acts, the defense reacts; the offense punches, the defense counterpunches. Attack football had sprung something new in the T formation. Now the defense had to realign to meet the threat of the T.

Part of the defense's difficulty lay in its inability to cope with the fast blocking utilized by the offensive line. Those brush blocks were murdering the linebackers; once the ball carrier squirmed through, only the two linebackers were there to stop him. If one was blocked out, that left a gaping hole, because the wing men were too far away, and they had to worry about passes anyhow. So the line dropped off one man to play "middle guard." Basically, the new defense became a 5–3–2–1 setup. And it seemed to work well for a while. Brush blocking lost its effectiveness, because the ball carrier was faced with three men behind the line instead of two, and one of them was right there to close the hole quickly.

But as the 1940's merged into the 1950's, the football geniuses spotted another weakness in the defense; the 5–3–2–1 was a sucker for deep passes. After all, there was only the single safety man out there. The linebackers were busy preventing short passes and shots into the line; the wingmen had the two ends to contend with. If only the offense could generate a little more manpower, to throw two potential receivers over the middle, deep. One could be a running back; but, to make the threat more effective, the second receiver had to be closer to the line.

The brain trusts began monkeying with the T formation a bit more, and what they came up with was the "third end" concept. That was the right halfback. No longer would he run with the ball as a running back. He became the new *flanker*.

The problem of where to put the new flanker turned out to be no problem at all, because he could be positioned almost anywhere, just so long as he was behind the line of scrimmage. He might be stationed wide of the tight end or in one of the slots between split end and tackle, or between tight end and tackle, or even wide of the split end. It made no difference, because everything depended on the play being run. Now there were three receivers in or near the line. More than ever before, pro football became a passing game.

In the old days a star passer such as Luckman or Baugh or Cecil Isbell was the exception rather than the rule. But as the midcentury mark was reached, the great passers began to flood the scene. They included such worthies as Otto Graham, Bob Waterfield, Y. A. Tittle, Norm Van Brocklin, and Bobby Layne.

Once upon a time great receivers were hard to come by. Gaynell Tinsley, Don Hutson, and Kenny Kavanaugh were the cream of the crop then (as they would be today). Now the host of long-legged, whippet-fast pass catchers arrived in abundance: Mac Speedie, Pete Pihos, Elroy "Crazy Legs" Hirsch, Tom Fears, Dante Lavelli, Billy Howton, and others.

Naturally, the passing game also needed the balance of a good running attack, just to keep the defense honest. Not every play was a pass, even though it sometimes seemed that way to the harried secondary. The good ball carriers, such as Marion Motley, Joe Perry, Hugh McElhenny, came up in profusion. These backs could also catch a football pretty well, in addition to blocking for the quarterback.

None of the new offensive patterns could have succeeded without improved playing techniques by the offensive line. The rules still insisted on seven players at the line of scrimmage, so there was no fooling around with new formations. But the way those interior linemen executed their assignments was a joy to behold.

On pass plays, the guards and tackles and center would raise up after the center-quarterback exchange and begin to form the "pass pocket." Some would join the backs in an arc around the passer and stand there, waiting for the inevitable pass rush. The rest of the line would try to hold back the incoming defensive linemen and linebackers. Planting their legs firmly, keeping their arms close to the body, elbows out, and fists at chest level, they would take the first blow, stagger back, take another blow, and keep trying to block out the defense until the passer got rid of the football.

On running plays they executed "angle blocks" with murderous effect, cutting the legs from under their defensive opponents. When an end sweep was called, the guards pulled out, ran parallel to the line of scrimmage, and turned the corner, wiping out the defensive ends and corner linebackers.

As the years passed, the offensive coaches kept experimenting with new wrinkles in attack formations. Sometimes they had limited success, as with the "shotgun" formation, a kind of short punt alignment. It was good for passing but weaker than normal for running. Other formations and gimmicks were more successful, including the formation and the "movable pass pocket." Also, the receivers refined their fakes and feints to a precision edge.

All these alterations took time and were put into operation over a period of years. Fundamentally, however, the damage had been done when the third end came in. That passing attack was tearing up the defense. Once again the counterpunch had to be thrown.

The 5–3–2–1 was obsolete, that much was certain. One safety man couldn't cope with the passes over the middle, just beyond the linebackers. Two safety men were mandatory. But where would the extra man come from?

Poring over their charts and tables, the defensive coaches came to the conclusion that the front line might be able to spare a player without getting hurt too badly. After all, the linebackers weren't *that* far away from scrimmage. A run of 40 or 50 yards didn't happen very often, but plenty of pass plays were gaining that much yardage. So the two ends and two tackles were left at the line and they became the modern *front four*. The middle guard became the middle linebacker; there were three permanent spots behind scrimmage. And the extra man was dropped all the way back to reinforce the single safety man. There were two deep defensive players. The new alignment was 4–3–2–2. To a great extent that's what it is today.

Formations by themselves mean nothing. The players make or break a team, regardless of how they line up. The new responsibilities of the front four required a new breed of defensive player, and they came into the pro ranks.

First, the defensive ends and tackles needed size, weight, and strength. The offensive line was very big too, and the front four somehow had to get through it. In the 1930's, a 210-pound lineman was considered heavy enough. But anyone that light couldn't take the punishment. No one could qualify for the defensive-end position unless he weighed a minimum of 235 or 240 pounds, and many were much heavier. The tackles started at 250 pounds, and in some rare instances (such as Roger Brown and Ernie Ladd) they went all the way up past the 300-pound mark. The heft was needed for several reasons:

To break through the pass pocket surrounding the quarterback, who had retreated about six or seven yards. Eventually, by running around a blocker, almost any player can reach through. But football is more scientific than many people think, and someone came up with fairly exact figures on the time it takes for a pass play to run its course: three and one-half seconds! In those brief clock-ticks, the quarterback takes the ball from center, drops back, sets, looks for his receiver, and throws. If you're a quarterback, that's not enough time, and if you're a lineman, that's an eternity. The defensive four use hands and heft and all kinds of strong-arm tactics to break in on the passer.

To stop the ground attack. On end sweeps, it is the responsibility of the defensive end (often helped by a corner linebacker) to turn in the ball carrier and prevent him from going around the corner along the sidelines. Usually he can't make the tackle himself, but if he can strip away the blocking, then it's fairly certain that the linebacker or the nearby tackle can make the grab. The tackles' responsibility on ground plays is to stop the straight-ahead off-tackle thrusts, to blunt them, strip the blocking, and let a teammate knock down the ball carrier. Some tackles can knock away blockers and ball carrier. Some years ago there was a huge mountain of a man named Gene "Big Daddy" Lipscomb, who developed a simple, straightforward philosophy that seemed to work—for him. Said Big Daddy, "I just bust in and tackle everybody in the backfield. Then I sort 'em out and keep the guy with the football."

Second, the defensive line had to be fast. Athletes will tell you that there are two kinds of speed: the type that enables a man to cover ground through sheer quickness of foot; and the type of trigger reflexes that enable him to "get off the ball" fast, to be inside the opposing line before the blocking can get set. The defensive lineman needs both types. Today it is not at all unusual to see a towering figure chase a sleek, swift ball carrier laterally across the field, catch him, and dump the running back for a loss!

Third—and far from least important—the front four had to be smart, always thinking, always trying to outfox the enemy. Sheer size and quickness aren't always enough. The opposing linemen aren't midgets—in fact they usually match the defensive line pretty well in the weight department. And despite the fact that an offensive lineman can't use his hands, the battle isn't as one-sided as the average spectator might think.

Sometimes an offensive lineman grabs his opponent's jersey and hangs on for a second or two, just long enough to delay the pass rush. Illegal? Sure! But the officials can't look everywhere at the same time, and often enough the holding isn't spotted.

Or, the offensive lineman can suddenly drop down, spin around and "leg-whip" a member of the charging front four. Many a defensive lineman has had his legs cut out from under him just when he thinks he's home free, and down he goes in a twisted heap. Plenty of front four knee cartilege has been torn up by those tactics.

And besides, those offensive linemen are pretty big and strong. It just isn't humanly possible to overpower them all the time.

So the defensive four learns to "juke," or stunt around. Instead of the right tackle running straight in, the right end may suddenly hit into the tackle's opponent, while the tackle loops around his teammate. There is a lot of feinting going on all the time.

Still, the defensive four learned that size, speed, and smartness weren't enough. They could be fooled so many different ways, by screen passes and draw plays, by fakes, and two-on-one blocking. After all was said and done, after game plans had been studied and worked out, the game of football boiled down to one violent credo:

Get the Quarterback!

All the great receivers and their intricate pass patterns, and all the fakes and feints by the running backs, and all the screen passes and draw plays would be just so much exercise in futility if the quarterback were dumped before he could throw the ball. Take away the passing game and the offense loses over half its effectiveness.

Or, to put it more crudely, kill the head and the body dies! The quarterback in modern pro football is the brains of the offense. Get rid of him and his big gun, the pass, and the rest of the attack will sputter out.

The front four specialize in reaching the passer. The best of them will pile in on the quarterback and batter him down as many as forty-five or fifty times during a fourteen-game season. Thus, at least three times during a game, the passer will have to eat the ball and pray he isn't killed while he lies on the ground under a pileup of defensive players.

That doesn't count the number of times a quarterback is so rushed, so harassed, that he throws the ball away, hoping that it won't be intercepted. Often enough his pass is picked off by the enemy.

In pro football circles they say that sooner or later all quarterbacks suffer from the occupational hazard known as "hearing the patter of little feet." After a few seasons of being pounded into the turf and having their teeth rattled by the charging front fours, the passers start listening for pounding footsteps coming their way. Sometimes they only think they hear the ground rumbling underfoot, but it bothers them just the same. Psychological or not, they have every reason to feel like innocent lambs staked out in tiger country. Who wouldn't quake and quail at the thought of half a ton of human destruction bearing down on him?

Great front fours do not make championship teams. Some of the best defensive lines in pro football have played on teams that lost consistently. But one thing is certain—no team ever won a championship without a solid front line defense. It's the same in every game; you can't win if the other team scores more points than you do.

Over the years there have been many great defensive linemen sprinkled through the ranks of football teams. This is the story of some of the best linemen in the game, who were fortunate enough to play on the same team at the same time.

Landry's Legions

OF ALL THE TEAMS IN PROFESSIONAL FOOTball, the New York Giants have the proudest championship heritage. This is not opinion but statistical fact. From 1933, when the first pro football championship game was played, through the Super Bowl game after the 1969 season, National Football League teams have participated in forty-one championship games of one sort or another. The Giants have competed in fourteen, more than either the Chicago Bears or Green Bay Packers, the two closest runners-up.

There are bound to be some nay-sayers who will discount that record as mere numbers picked out of a hat. After all, the Giants never played in a Super Bowl game, while the Packers were entries twice and won both. That's true. And they might also be quick to point out that the Giants' championship record is pretty sad, for they won three and lost eleven. That's also true.

However, it also helps to remember that in order to get into a league championship game, a team must first win a divisional title, and that's not exactly easy. The Giants did it fourteen times. Green Bay won ten NFL divisional championships and two Super Bowl games, a total of twelve. Chicago reached the top ten times (no Super Bowl games). Any questions?

Both Green Bay and Chicago have fielded outstanding defensive units—and so have the Giants. In 1934, for example, New York had a forward wall second to none, keystoned by Mel Hein, who was certainly among the half-dozen greatest centers to play pro football. In the championship game against Chicago, Hein, along with Butch Gibson and Tom Jones at guards, played the entire sixty minutes in a winning cause. They had to stop a raging fullback named Bronco Nagurski, who chewed up linemen the way kids today chomp bubble gum. And they stopped him!

In 1944, the Giants had another outstanding lineman, Al Blozis. When they played Green Bay (and lost, 14–7), Blozis put on a demonstration of line play that left even opposing fans cheering his courage and determination. After the game, Blozis reported to his army unit and shipped out for the combat zone. He was killed in Belgium a month later, leading an assault on an enemy machine-gun nest.

Following their participation in the 1946 playoff game against Chicago—and, incidentally, they lost again—the Giants fell upon evil days. They went up and down in the standings like a yo-yo. In 1947, the former divisional champions were in last place; the next year they were third, but posted a 4–8–0 record. Then followed some fairly decent years and some poor ones. The team floundered, showing promise but never fulfillment. Something was lacking. Call it fighting spirit, call it precision or execution; whatever it was, it just wasn't there.

In 1954, the Giants had a new head coach. Jim Lee Howell replaced Steve Owen, who had held the reins since 1931. And what happened later was, in a sense, peculiar; in time the Giants achieved a reputation as one of pro football's finest defensive teams. Yet Steve Owen had been the one who stressed defense, while Howell leaned toward stronger offense. In comparing the two coaches, a New York sportswriter noted that Owen was the type who would be happy winning by a 3–0 score, while Howell would be pleased if the score were 38–35—in favor of the Giants, naturally.

As assistants, Howell hired two men who were to change the entire concept of football. The offensive coach was Vince Lombardi; it would be considered almost un-American today for even a nonsports fan to admit that he never heard of Lombardi. The defensive coach was a member of the Giants' defensive secondary, Tom Landry. Later, Howell was to cite Landry as the greatest innovator and the finest defensive coach in football. It was Landry, more than anyone else, who helped to solidify the concept of a 4–3 defense.

Landry didn't begin his career as a defensive genius. He was an all-regional high school fullback in Texas, and after service in World War II as a B-17 pilot (thirty missions over enemy territory) he returned home to attend the University of Texas. Landry played varsity ball for three years. In his junior year he was second-string quarterback and saw little action. No wonder. The starting quarterback was Bobby Layne, and no hot-shot *pro* passer ever took away his job either. Landry went back to the fullback position and did pretty well.

He had started his professional football career with the New York Yankees of the All-America Conference, and when that league folded, he hooked on with the Giants in 1950. He was to stay with them as player and coach for ten years. Landry, Otto Schnellbacher, Harmon Rowe, and Em Tunnell formed Steve Owen's "Umbrella Defense," which was a stopgap measure designed to thwart the enemy passing attack.

It was the defense set up by Paul Brown of the Cleveland Browns that influenced Landry's thinking to a great extent. In the early 1950's, Cleveland was the ranking power in professional football, winning *six consecutive divisional titles* and three of the championship games. Brown was a brilliant general, and the players were his shock troops, responding to his commands on cue. He sent in nearly all the offensive plays, and he directed the defense to exploit the enemy weaknesses his keen mind and eyes spotted. In his own mind Landry found himself improving on Brown's concepts, going a step further.

But he wrought no overnight changes, mostly because he did not have the personnel he wanted. Two unproductive years, 1954 and 1955, passed; both seasons the Giants finished third. Then, as if someone had waved a magic wand, Landry had the horses. His great defense arrived all at once—or so it seemed. All of a sudden, in 1956, Landry's Legions included Andy Robustelli, Roosevelt Grier, Jim Katcavage, Dick Modzelewski and Sam Huff.

The inclusion of Sam Huff with the others—all defensive linemen—might seem out of order in the light of football in the 4–3 alignment. But even as late as 1956, Huff was listed in the lineup as "middle guard." Two years later, in the printed lineup for a championship game between the Giants and Baltimore Colts, Huff was called "middle linebacker," and the change was not merely one of nomenclature.

Robustelli was the newcomer with the most previous experience. Handy Andy had spent five years with the Los Angeles Rams before being traded to the Giants, and Landry saw in him a natural leader, a teacher, and above all a great fighting spirit.

Robustelli was a product of Stamford High School and tiny Arnold College, both in Connecticut. The Arnold team never received much attention in the newspapers because the school's enrollment was so small (350 students, 70 of them girls) that there were only similar small schools on its schedule. It bumped heads with such teams as Kings Point, New Haven Teachers, Wagner, and the Coast Guard Academy. Probably Robustelli would have become a physical-education teacher if it had not been for a Los Angeles scout named Red Hickey who liked to poke into small colleges looking for talent.

The Arnold game that Hickey saw was peculiar. Andy made a

lot of tackles, blocked a couple of kicks—and broke his leg! But Hickey sensed a potential great one in Robustelli, and recommended that the Rams give him a tryout. Accordingly, Andy became their nineteenth draft choice, which is right next door to being a free agent.

Robustelli went to California in 1951, hoping to catch on as an offensive or defensive end. Then he took one look at the offensive receivers and realized there was no way he could oust anybody. Prancing around were Crazy Legs Hirsch, Tom Fears, and Bob Boyd, three of the fastest pass catchers in the business. Sick at heart, Robustelli didn't even unpack his bags for two weeks, expecting the axe to fall at any moment. But coach Joe Stydahar encouraged him to stay, saying that he might still make it as a defensive end. Andy kept plugging away, and he made it. In 1956 he went to New York in exchange for a future No. 1 draft pick. From nineteenth draft pick to first—that's a big jump in any league!

Next in the Giant front four seniority was Dick "Little Mo" Modzelewski. Little Mo came from an athletics-oriented family. His older brother, Ed (Big Mo), was a fullback with the Cleveland Browns, and his brother Joe was a boxer and stablemate of the former heavyweight champion Ezzard Charles. Dick attended the University of Maryland and was drafted by the Washington Redskins in 1953. But he saw little service for two years and was dealt off to Pittsburgh, where he remained for one year before the Giants obtained him.

The nicknames Big Mo and Little Mo were completely misleading. They referred to age, not size. Big Mo, the fullback, was two years older and weighed 220 pounds; Little Mo, the tackle, stood 6 feet 1 inch and weighed 250!

Grier and Katcavage were rookies.

Roosevelt Grier was a veritable monster of a human being. Rearing up at 6 feet 5 inches and ranging between 285 and 315 pounds during his career, the Penn State star looked like a walking building. In a game, he hit quarterbacks and ball carriers with awesome power, but off the field he was a gentle, guitar-playing funny man who would talk about his poverty-stricken boyhood, when he often ate salt-and-pepper sandwiches to stave off the pangs of hunger.

Jim Katcavage, a 6-foot 3-inch 240-pounder from the University of Dayton, made it to pro football because of a surgeon's skill. He had been a pretty good high school basketball player, but one year he dislocated his shoulder six times! College scouts weren't enthusiastic about a kid with a shoulder that popped out every time someone shoved him hard. Jim submitted to an operation after he was graduated from high school in 1952. The surgeon took out the shoulder joint, scraped the bone, then shortened and knotted together the ligaments. It was a master's piece of work; the shoulder never caused trouble again. Katcavage did quite well at Dayton. In his rookie year with the Giants, he shared the defensive-end position with a holdover veteran named Walt Yowarsky.

The long first-place drought came to an end in 1956, when the Giants won their first divisional title in ten years. Then they drubbed the Chicago Bears in the playoff game. It wasn't even close. The defensive line rushed the passer, stopped the running attack, and New York had an easy 47–7 victory. Chicago managed to gain a mere sixty-seven yards on the ground.

New York's front four was temporarily broken up in 1957 when Rosey Grier went into the Army. Katcavage filled in at tackle. The Giants finished second, and that seemed to prove conclusively the value of the entire line as a unit. In a way it was disconcerting, because an injury to any one of the four—one that forced a lineman out for several games—could mean the difference between first place and also-ran.

The return of Rosey Grier in 1958 didn't signal an immediate return to the top. Somehow the gears wouldn't mesh, the team stuttered and stumbled, and by mid-October the Giants were two games behind the Cleveland Browns. But they suddenly settled down and went into a homestretch drive. New York beat Cleveland in a "must" game and took off on a dash for the top, keeping pace with the Browns. The race came down to the wire with the season's finale spelling the difference. As luck would have it, the game was against Cleveland.

It was a stiff test. If the Giants won, they'd tie the Browns. That would mean another showdown game for the Eastern title. They had already beaten Cleveland once during the season; asking them to do it twice more seemed too much.

But they came through! In the first encounter, New York squeezed it out, 13–10. And in the decider it was 10–0. The Giants' defense was magnificent. In eleven previous games, Cleveland's powerful offensive unit had scored 292 points; Robustelli and the other stalwarts held them to ten points in two games! New York sportswriters called Howell's boys "The Cinderella Team," and the defensive line was "Landry's Legions."

The championship game against Baltimore is now firmly established as "The Greatest Game Ever Played." The defense of both teams was magnificent, with each putting on determined stands to stop the other. Perhaps the most dramatic defensive play came in the third quarter, when the Colts led, 14–3. They had possession on the 1-yard line, with four tries to push over another touchdown. If they scored, the Giants would probably never recover.

Three times the Baltimore backfield powered into the line, and three times the runners bounced back as Rosey Grier and Little Mo refused to budge an inch. On fourth down the Giant linebacker Cliff Livingston slithered through, chased down Alan "The Horse" Ameche, and dropped him on the 5-yard line.

Thus inspired, New York stormed back and took a 17–14 lead. Late in the game Baltimore put on a drive that will be remembered for years to come as a perfect match-up between a great quarterback against a tough defensive line. Landry's Legions tried desperately to stop Johnny Unitas and they got in on him a couple of times. But in the end he prevailed. Johnny U took the Colts into field-goal range, and on the last play of the game in regulation time, Steve Myhra booted the 3-pointer that forced a sudden-death overtime period.

The Giants took the kickoff, and fine work by the Baltimore line stopped them. The Colts took the punt and started rolling from their own 20. In practically no time they were on their own 41.

The Legions dug in. A run was stopped for no gain. Then the line roared in and dropped Johnny U for a loss of 5. Unitas hit Ray Berry with a pass good for 21 yards. A draw play gained only a yard, and then a line smash yielded exactly nothing. Unitas hit again with a pass to the 8-yard line. Ameche bucked for only a yard, but a pass to the sideline put the ball on New York's 1-yard line. Finally the Horse rammed it over, going through a hole wide enough for a locomotive.

In defeat the Giants had nothing to be ashamed of. Unitas, Ameche, the Baltimore players, coaches, sportswriters, and fans saluted Howell's club as one of the finest all-around groups ever assembled. The Colt ball carriers lavished particular praise on the defensive line, calling it one of the best in football history.

With another year of experience under their belts, the still-young Giant defensive linemen figured to be even better in 1959. And they were. But they also needed a little scare to cure them of their overconfidence. That came in the second game of the season.

After beating Los Angeles by 23–21, Howell's boys ran into the Philadelphia Eagles and a whiplash arm attached to a fellow named Norm Van Brocklin. When the shouting had died away, the Giants were still trying to get the license number of the truck that had hit them. Van Brocklin and his cohorts ripped the Giant defenses into rag scraps, and the 49–21 pasting absorbed by the Giants was the worst since the 62–14 defeat by Cleveland in 1953.

That jolt seemed to snap the defense to its senses. It bounced back, handing Cleveland a 10–6 beating, and then in a rematch with Van Brocklin, took him over the hurdles, 24–7. At that, the Eagles had to fight for their lives to get their lone touchdown. Philadelphia had the ball on New York's 1-yard line, first and goal. Billy Barnes tried the middle and got nowhere. Clarence Peaks slashed forward and was stopped. Van Brocklin attempted a sneak and gained 12 inches. Barnes finally took it across on the fourth and final try. After that, Landry Legions shut the touchdown door. Philadelphia gained only 68 yards rushing. The Giant line harassed Van Brocklin all day.

Ro and Mo and Rosey and Jim put on another great exhibition of line play in the next game, against Pittsburgh. This time they faced another old pro named Bobby Layne. With the Giants leading, 21–16, and less than 2 minutes to go, all-pro Ernie Stautner recovered a Giant fumble on the New York 16. Layne promptly fired a pass to Buddy Dial, who was tackled just short of the 6-yard line. The Steelers needed less than a yard, and there was plenty of time.

Three times Tom Tracy slammed into the line, and he never did make it. The final try left the running back inches short. But the Giant line had been doing that to the Pittsburgh ball-carriers all day. The Steelers got 33 yards rushing in 60 minutes of football.

One particular play in New York's 20–3 victory over Green Bay showed how well the New York line and the rest of the defense worked together. The Packers had possession deep in their own territory. In the Giants' defensive huddle, linebacker Harland Svare whispered "Blitz Wanda." At the snap, Robustelli went wide intsead of charging straight ahead, luring the offensive tackle with him. Svare went through the hole left by the tackle and belted the Green Bay running back, Don McIlhenny, just as he took off. McIlhenny fumbled, and Little Mo recovered on the Packer 3!

The Cardinals, then operating out of Chicago, fell before

Lombardi's Blocks of Granite

IT'S FUNNY HOW PEOPLE LEARN THINGS from other people. Even the specialists, the experts. Sometimes it's by osmosis. A man learns a new skill, or polishes his old one, almost in spite of himself. It's not a reasoning act; all of a sudden, he has a new way of thinking.

Of course there are those who learn deliberately, by observation, concentration, and dedication. They have one expertise to begin with, then they add a few ingredients, muddle them all together, let the pot stew for a year or two, and the result is something different. That's the Vince Lombardi method.

Even before he died on September 2, 1970, Lombardi was a legend, big as life and twice as tough. Those who served under him called Lombardi a slave driver, a martinet, a mob leader, and a few other choice epithets. Maybe he was all of them and more. But he was also a first-rate football coach, among the innovators, ranking with all the others who put their personal stamp on the game of football.

of the line when necessary, but still basically operating in the middle secondary. There would be many more such defensive fours to follow; but that, as they say, is a whole flock of other stories.

point came in the third quarter, and it all hinged on a single play.

The Giants had the ball on the Colt 28, with a fourth-and-1 situation confronting the Giant offense. They led, 9–7; a touchdown would ease the pressure, give them confidence, for they had not been able to put the ball over the Colt goal line. Alex "Red" Webster took the handoff and was cruelly embraced at the line of scrimmage by Big Daddy Lipscomb and Gino Marchetti, who dropped him in his tracks. Baltimore took over and broke the game open with 24 fourth-quarter points. New York did score later, when it didn't matter. The final score was 31–16.

And then Tom Landry was gone. A new NFL franchise was being formed in Dallas—the team was tentatively called Rangers but was soon changed to Cowboys. Landry was buttonholed, sweet-talked, and signed. Lombardi had switched over to Green Bay the year before. Thus the great staff of assistant coaches was gone.

Landry had done his work well. In 1958 and 1959 the Giants were defensive leaders, having yielded the fewest points of any team in the NFL. Since several teams outscored them, obviously defense had won the conference titles. After Landry left, the Giants continued to do well. They slid to third place in 1960, when Philadelphia copped the honors and Cleveland finished second for the third time in succession. After that, New York ripped off a string of three more eastern championships.

But 1963 was the last good year of the decade. By trade and retirement, Landry's Wrecking Crew was broken up. Grier was dealt to Los Angeles, Little Mo to Cleveland; Robustelli quit and then Kat.

Tom Landry's Giant front four was special for two reasons. First, of course, it was a great line. The records speak for themselves. And second, it was really the first outstanding set of defensive linemen to operate under the 4–3 system of four guys up front with three men backing them up, moving in and out

New York, 9–3. For the second game in a row, the Giants had not yielded a touchdown, only two field goals, one in each game. The last time that feat had been accomplished, five years before, Detroit's great line had pulled the trick.

Then followed a heart-breaking 14–9 loss to Bobby Layne's Steelers. Pittsburgh scored the winning touchdown with just 1:29 left on the clock.

But nobody dared blame the New York line. The Giants had accumulated nine points against the Cardinals and nine more against Pittsburgh. There were no touchdowns scored, only six field goals. Those three-point shots were mighty handy, but they couldn't keep winning ballgames all the time. Yet it wasn't altogether the fault of the offensive unit either. At one time or another Charlie Conerly, Kyle Rote, and Frank Gifford were injured, and the Giants had to go with subs a good deal.

The line stood up well against the Cardinals in the following game. Although there was plenty of scoring, New York won, 30–20—one Cardinal touchdown was the result of a 60-yard runback of a Giant punt.

And in the Giants' 45–14 rout of the Redskins, Washington's two touchdowns came as a result of Giant fumbles. But even then Landry's Legions were just coasting. The score was 38–0 at the half, why rub it in?

New York won the divisional title in the game against Cleveland. The defensive line's domination of the Brownie attack was total, complete, entire. Even the 48–7 score wasn't indicative of what happened. The great Jimmy Brown was held to fifty yards in fifteen carries, and the rest of Cleveland's rushing attack gained only sixty yards more. The only Cleveland score came on a seventy-eight-yard punt return by the fleet Bobby Mitchell.

It would be nice to report that the New York Giants avenged themselves against Baltimore, but it didn't turn out that way. For three periods the Giants threw a scare into Unitas and company, but then the game fell apart. Probably the turning

With the Giants, it seemed that Lombardi might have been out of place. He should have had Tom Landry's job and vice versa. For Landry had been an offensive back in college, and had to make the switch to defense with the pros. Lombardi was a defensive lineman at Fordham University, one of the noted "Seven Blocks of Granite" who held off the foe in the 1930's. He wasn't big, but he was savage. There are those who say the word "fight" wasn't in the dictionary until he invented it. That was the simple basic quality he instilled in his players. Even more than sheer excellence, he demanded all-out effort 100 per cent of the time. Anyone giving less was begging to be traded.

Yet it was Tom Landry who put it into quotable words: "You can't teach defense unless you also know all about offense." And it was Vince Lombardi, the defensive player and offensive coach, who combined the two in his own way. He installed a kind of "defensive offense." Some called it ball-control, others maintained that Lombardi had just gone back to the traditional basics of sound tackling, blocking, and ball carrying. Maybe everybody was right.

Lombardi almost didn't get to Green Bay. A year before he accepted the Packer job, Philadelphia came to him with a very generous offer. Lombardi mulled it over for a while and turned it down. Perhaps it was just as well, for the Eagles skidded to the bottom in 1958, in spite of all Buck Shaw's efforts.

Green Bay was desperate when its front office began negotiations with Lombardi. For two years the Packers had kept a death grip on the cellar, the 1958 season having been a special disaster. They slunk home with a 1–10–1 record, and the statistics showed why. The team scored fewer points and permitted more points to be scored against it than any other in the league. That's really more unusual than it sounds. In 1957, for example, the Packers scored 218 points, while the Chicago Bears, who finished one rung higher, scored only 203 points.

Lombardi agreed to take the job only if he could run the

team with a free hand. He would brook no interference from the front office. The executives figured they had nothing to lose. In six years the Packers had finished last three times, next-to-last twice, and third once. Some wits declared that the front office was so far out on a limb that it would have agreed to those terms even if they had been proposed by Mickey Mouse.

Lombardi attacked his assignment with the zeal of a housewife doing her spring cleaning. Anybody who disagreed with him, for any reason whatever, was out. He demanded utter obedience. As Henry Jordan, a defensive tackle, said later, "When Lombardi says sit down, I don't even look for a chair. I sit!"

Years of training as a Fordham lineman and his keen observations of Landry's front four had given Lombardi a good idea of the type of player he wanted.

One of them was already a Green Bay mainstay. Dave "Hawg" Hanner had been drafted fifth by Green Bay in 1952. When his coaches learned that the 6-foot 2-inch, 260-pound gentle giant was Packer-bound, they almost wept for him. Their pity was wasted. Hanner was the type who never learned to accept defeat, no matter how often he tasted it—and that was pretty often. He played with aches and pains, he played when the odds looked hopeless, he played his heart out for the perennial cellar dwellers. Not counting exhibitions, he played in 110 straight games before an appendectomy laid him low. Hanner missed exactly one game! Obviously, he was Lombardi's kind of guy.

The new coach set about accumulating additional fighters. But where were they? Well, most likely on a winning team, perhaps impatiently picking up bench splinters. And which team was always right up there in the thick of the fight? Why, Cleveland, of course. So Lombardi peeked at the Cleveland roster, stuck a pin into a pair of names, and came away with two beauties for the 1959 season. Their names were Bill Quinlan and Henry Jordan. Quinlan was very much put out at the idea of joining a crew of tail-enders. Jordan would have hooked up with anybody who offered him a chance to play regularly, and been thankful for the opportunity.

Quinlan, 6 feet 3 inches and 250 pounds of fighting muscle, was a bit of a troublemaker—of the best kind, of course. He loved to needle people, to get into everybody's hair, to rile them. When he arrived at the Green Bay camp he noted that the air was thick with gloom, and that was something he couldn't stand. They'd never get out of the cellar that way. So he boasted and bragged and in general made himself obnoxious. Nearly everyone ignored Quinlan, but not Hawg Hanner.

"Hey, Hanner," roared Quinlan, "I'm an end, but I'll bet I can play tackle better than you. In fact I'll bet I'm a better everything than you."

Hanner flushed and got up. "Wanna find out?" he asked quietly. Quinlan laughed mightily. "That's the way to talk!" he shouted "Now you look like a football player!" The Packers understood immediately. Quinlan played football the way Lombardi demanded it be played. Everybody up, everybody ready to fight, everybody wins! In fact, since his Michigan State days, Big Bill Quinlan had never played on a losing team, and he wasn't about to begin with Green Bay.

Even at Michigan State, Quinlan had been a rough-and-tumble character. He was a member of the team when it went to the Rose Bowl, and when it took honors as the mythical college champion. But he did more than play football. While the team was in Pasadena, California, during the Rose Bowl festivities, a hotel caught fire. Quinlan carried a number of elderly people to safety, including a man in a wheel chair. He took no bows.

Quinlan didn't finish college. He was expelled for a typical reason—fighting. He spent some time in Canada, playing with the Hamilton, Ontario, Tigers. From there he went to the Browns, and now the Packers had him.

Jordan, 6 feet 2 inches and 245 pounds, had been Cleveland's fifth draft choice in 1957, from the University of Virginia. The Browns never did find out his full potential because seemingly they had better players to fill the regular spots. Jordan was used on all the special teams—the kickoff team, the field-goal team, the goal-line team. But not the regular team. Given a chance to play with the first-stringers, Jordan exceeded even Lombardi's expectations.

Jordan, realizing he didn't have the heft and power to knock over the bigger offensive linemen, relied on brains, guile, and observation. Of course, when he *had to* outfight an opponent, Jordan could do that too; he'd been a great wrestler in college.

To show how Jordan operated:

When Big Jim Parker was on the Baltimore scene at offensive guard, getting through to Unitas was a feat comparable to climbing Mount Everest. Jordan did it. He didn't go around Parker or over him—he went through Parker's legs!

And he psyched the opposition dizzy. Crouching down at the line, he once said to an opponent, "I'm so tired and hurting, I think I'll faint. Go easy on me, huh?" Then, with the snap of the ball—whoosh! He was by the startled lineman so fast he seemed blurred.

In another game, he faced a smart old pro and figured that his best bet was to go outside. But the veteran kept shoving him to the inside time after time. Afterward, studying the game films, he spotted his mistake. Jordan had lined up with his right foot three inches farther back than normal. The old pro had obviously studied Jordan's previous games with a magnifying glass and he knew instantly what Jordan intended to do. The prematurely bald Jordan grinned ruefully, scratched the skin on his head, and vowed never to tip his hand like that again.

Under Lombardi's command, improvement was dramatic. From last place the Packers went to third. From a 1–10–1 record, they went to 7–5–0. Whereas the defense had allowed 382 points, now the opposition scored 246. The offense was greatly improved too, 193 up to 248. Lombardi had indeed revitalized the team.

The following year Green Bay made it to the top of the division. In part this was due to the addition of a defensive end, Willie Davis. To get him, Lombardi went shopping at the same store in Cleveland.

A 6-foot 3-inch product of Grambling College in Louisiana, Davis was a really fine student in math and industrial arts. Evidently Cleveland didn't think much of him as a student of football, for he was shipped off to Green Bay in exchange for another spare lineman, A. D. Williams. In a way, Lombardi was taking a chance, for Davis had been passing himself off as an offensive player. Perhaps Lombardi felt that with a couple of extra pounds Willie could make the grade on defense. He did, too, with 240 pounds of pass-rushing lightning distributed on his frame.

This was the front four Vince Lombardi fielded in 1960. And it was the front four that helped him bring home a divisional title. The team got off to a bad start, righted itself, and with the help of other clubs in the league, which upset the front-running Colts, came out on top. In the pennant-winning game against the San Francisco 49ers, the defensive line put on a fantastic display of power. Not until twelve minutes of the third quarter did the 49ers reach the Green Bay forty-nine-yard line, and that was their deepest penetration!

Maybe a Hollywood screenwriter could have made a movie epic of the 1960 NFL championship game. Certainly all the ingredients were there. The Packers played the Eagles; Lombardi had been offered the coaching job with both clubs. In 1958, both teams had finished last in their respective divisions, and now they were at the top. Buck Shaw was a kindly old soul, Lombardi a stern, almost militaristic man. And the Eagles won, 17–13.

But it was far more than a cornball melodrama. This was a

crackling good game of football, and it wasn't so much that the Packers lost as the fact that time ran out on them. As sometimes happens in a close game, one series of plays made the difference.

Trailing by 13–10, the Eagles punched back swiftly, and about midway into the final period were on the Green Bay 20. As Norm Van Brocklin dropped back to pass, the entire Green Bay front four and two linebackers poured in on him, knocking him flat on the 27. The next play was bound to be a pass, and Van Brocklin obliged. Only he flipped a soft one to Billy Barnes, who threaded his way down to the 14, a 13-yard pickup.

Later, Willie Davis blamed himself for that gain. He had had no chance to stop the completion, but said that perhaps he hadn't given his pursuit that little extra something that would have stopped Barnes sooner. Nobody else thought so. But Davis was thoroughly Lombardi-conditioned.

Philadelphia scored a couple of plays later and then staved off a desperation Green Bay rally, which saw Jim Taylor swarmed under inside the Eagle 20 on the last play of the game.

As it turned out, Lombardi had merely traded one victory for many. Two years later Philadelphia was back in the cellar, while the Packers were being acclaimed as the cream of pro football. Perhaps the Eagles wouldn't have plummeted so fast had Lombardi been at the helm, because certainly the Pack went onward and upward.

The continued improvement in the Green Bay steamroller was simply too much. Statisticians can sometimes make numbers jump through a hoop to prove any point at all. But nobody could tamper with the Green Bay numbers because they were too fantastic.

In 1960, the first title year, the defense yielded 209 points in twelve games for a 17.4 average per game. The next year it was 223 points in fourteen games for a 16-point average. And in 1962, when Green Bay flaunted a 13–1–0 record, it was 148 points in fourteen games for a 10.6 average per game. Had it not been for a stunning upset at the hands of Detroit, the Packers would have gone undefeated and set all sorts of defensive records.

It might have been another grade-B Hollywood classic if Lombardi's Packers had clashed in a playoff game against the Giants of his former boss, Jim Lee Howell. Perhaps the fates *did* sort of lean in that direction, and the two teams did meet in the postseason game, not once but twice. But Howell was gone after 1960. In his place was another former New York assistant coach, Allie Sherman. Evidently the Giants were a great team to practice on, for Sherman was the third assistant to get his own team in the space of four years.

Both encounters were qiute properly billed as clashes between two powerhouses, offensively and defensively. Landry's Legions were still intact for the two games, and had been seasoned by a couple of added years of experience. The same held true for Lombardi's granite wall. The experts figured that the games might be decided by the breaks, and that's what happened.

For a full first period in the 1961 game, the teams probed and pushed and felt each other out. The Packers closed out the quarter on the New York 6-yard line, and 4 seconds into the second quarter, Paul Hornung went over right tackle for a touchdown. But 7–0 wasn't much of a lead, not with two great veterans such as Y. A. Tittle and Chuck Conerly passing for the Giants.

The first turn-around break came right after the Packer score. On third-and-6 from his own 30, Tittle dropped back to pass. Henry Jordan slithered through the protective cup and managed to tip the ball just as it left Y. A.'s hand. The ball flipped crazily into the air and was intercepted by a linebacker, Ray Nitschke, who returned it to the New York 34. In six plays the Packers had another touchdown.

Once more Tittle tried to get the Giants moving, only to be thwarted by the Packer line. Tittle's first passing attempt was fouled up when Willie Davis raced through to nail him. The second try fell incomplete. The third one precipitated such a rush that the Bald Eagle had to get rid of it anywhere at all, and unfortunately for the Giants, Green Bay's Hank Gremminger caught it. New York's defensive unit, which had just sat down on the bench, got up wearily and was ripped apart. Jim Taylor and Hornung carried to the 14, and then Bart Starr finished the job with a touchdown pass to Ron Kramer.

Desperately hoping to change the luck, Allie Sherman sent Conerly into replace Tittle, but for one play it seemed that the Packer line was playing no favorites in destroying the passer. As Conerly went through the passing motion, with a receiver out in the clear, Hawg Hanner got through and hit his arm. The ball fell harmlessly to the ground. Conerly regrouped his forces and did get the Giants moving. They reached the Packer 6. But on fourth down an option pass missed connections, and Green Bay took over.

From then on, it was all downhill for New York. The Packers added a field goal and walked into the locker room at halftime leading by 24–0. The Giants were licked; even the hot-dog hawkers knew that much. All that remained was to see how bad the beating would be, and whether the Giants would score at all.

Green Bay's front line never let up. When the Giants got the ball in the third period, they ran just three plays and had to punt. On the first play, Conerly's flare pass to Alex Webster lost 5. Webster tried a center draw on the second play and lost another 5. Conerly hit Joe Walton with a pass good for 18 yards, but that was still 2 yards shy of a first down, so New York's defensive crew was back on the field before they could rest their weary bones. And they held, forcing Green Bay to punt.

But Joe Morrison fumbled the kick, Green Bay recovered, and back came the exhausted defensive unit.

Again the men of Landry's Legions held, but the Packers

had regained possession too close to be denied another score. Hornung split the uprights from the 22.

The Packers showed no mercy. The line dropped Tittle twice, once for a loss of 6, then for a loss of 9. He couldn't take a deep breath without seeing Packers all around him. It was a 37–0 nightmare.

Yet Landry's Legions had not been disgraced. They just wore out from playing so much. In the fourth quarter, for instance, they held the Packers in check on one series, forcing a punt. Hoping desperately for a score, Tittle passed deep toward Del Shofner. But the Packers knew he'd pass—what else could he do? So the heave was intercepted. Thus the Giants had the ball for exactly one play, and their defensive unit was back on the field again.

However, that took nothing away from Green Bay's strong line. The Giants achieved only half a dozen first downs, and accumulated only thirty-one yards rushing. That's playing *great* defensive ball!

For a whole year the Giants brooded about that defeat. And when both teams repeated in their respective divisions, it seemed like an ideal time to put Vince Lombardi and his bully boys back into proper perspective. After all, they were due for a fall. Hadn't Detroit turned the trick on Thanksgiving Day? A good line, such as the Lions' or the Giants', could knock off the Packers. And what better time than in a championship game?

The first time Green Bay got its hands on the ball, it started a steady march designed to knock the Giants right out of Yankee Stadium. The Pack went all the way to the 20 before the Giant line stiffened, forcing Green Bay to settle for a field goal.

And then Landry's Wrecking Crew decided that this foolishness had gone on long enough. But luck still seemed to favor the Packers. Shortly after their score, a Tittle pass was deflected by Ray Nitschke and intercepted by Dan Currie. Green Bay couldn't convert that break into a score because Robustelli and

Little Mo and Grier and Katcavage zeroed in on Jim Taylor and began bouncing him around with merry spirits. On the last four plays of the first quarter, Taylor carried four times. He gained a grand total of 3 yards! Big Jim lost 1 at left end, gained 3 over center, was held to no gain at left end, and gained a yard at left tackle. Kramer's attempted field goal from the 37 was short and wide of the mark as the 25-mile-an-hour wind gave the Giants a little assist.

Green Bay didn't do too well the next time it gained possession. Hornung, Taylor, and Starr each got first downs, and it seemed as if the Pack had found the right road. But then Starr was creamed for a loss of 10, threw two harassed incompletions, and the Packers had to give up the football.

All credit to Lombardi's line; it held fast, too. And so did the Giants'. When Green Bay tried again and was faced with a third-and-3 situation, Starr decided against bucking the wind and fed the ball to his fullback. Instead of gaining 3, Taylor *lost* 3. He hit the frozen turf with a thud that could be heard in the last row of bleacher seats behind the goal posts.

But those fumbles—those giveaway fumbles—hurt the Giants again. Phil King lost the handle on New York's 28 and Nitschke found it. An option pass from Hornung to Boyd Dowler and a 7-yard run by Jim Taylor—the Giants couldn't stop him all the time—produced a touchdown.

For the first time in the two championship games, the Giants got on the scoreboard, but through no effort of the offensive unit. In the third period, Erich Barnes blocked a punt, Jim Collier recovered in the end zone, and the Giants had 7 points after the conversion.

All through that cold, windy, dreary day, those two marvelous defensive lines took turns beating up each other's offense. The Packer line kept pressuring Y.A. Tittle, and they were in on him so much he began to think they were part of his backfield. Bart Starr, trying to keep his precarious lead and eat up time, kept the ball on the ground, and the Giant line had a field day, tossing the Packer runners around like sacks of cement. On one fourth-quarter series, Jim Taylor gained 2 yards over left tackle and promptly lost them back in the same spot on the next play. Tom Moore lost 4 on a draw. So, three shots into the New York line produced a net *loss* of 4 yards.

But the defense could get no more points for New York, and the offense couldn't either. The Giants lost again, 16–7. But the defensive line had covered itself with glory, and nobody could take that away from them. Jim Taylor was almost an ambulance case after the game. He had carried the ball thirty-one times, but gained only an average of 2.7 yards per carry. When someone mentioned the number of carries, Big Jim licked at the bloody lip he sported and remarked wryly, "That means I was on the ground thirty-one times."

Fuzzy Thurston, Green Bay's all-pro offensive guard, said, "You could really feel it when they hit you out there today. You could feel it in your bones. Today the Giants were the best I've ever seen 'em."

Green Bay didn't win in 1963, in spite of another fine record. Nor did it take the honors in 1964. However, Lombardi's guys started all over again in 1965 and put together another skein of championships. By then Bill Quinlan was long gone and Hawg Hanner had retired. They were replaced by another great pair, Lionel Aldridge at end and Ron Kostelnik at tackle. Together with Jordan and Davis, and cemented by great linebackers, Vince Lombardi's granite blocks wrote great new chapters in the history of defensive football.

A Pride of Lions

THE AVERAGE FOOTBALL FAN IS UNDER THE impression that a great front four is composed of a quartet of equally talented players. That is not necessarily so. In football, as in any sport, some players are better than others, and some players work better together than others. There is no hard-and-fast rule. It would be much more accurate to describe a good front line as a group that knows how to exploit its strengths and minimize its slightly weaker elements.

Now, the word *weaker* calls for some explanation. Obviously, there are no mediocrities in professional football. A player who can't measure up to the position is cut, and that's the end of it. But there are gradations of talent. A man can be a superstar, or a very good player, or an average player. A standout front four can be made up of a couple of superstars and two "average" or slightly better men and still rank with the best. There are many variables, which are difficult to define or nail down accurately. Perhaps it is best to analyze one sequence of players and let the fan drawn his own conclusion. A good group would be the Detroit Lions foursome of 1959 to 1962.

In 1959, the starting front four of the Lions consisted of Bill Glass and Darris McCord at ends, and Alex Karras and Gil Mains at tackles. All were veterans.

Glass had played his college football at Baylor University, then spent a year playing in Canada before signing with the Lions. The 6-foot 6-inch former divinity student weighed a solid 255 pounds.

McCord, a former star at the University of Tennessee, was considered one of the most underrated defensive players in the NFL. He stood 6 feet 4 inches in sweat sox and tipped the scales at 250 pounds. Never known for great speed or overwhelming strength, McCord had an excellent football sense. He could read the offense and make the necessary adjustments quickly.

Mains was a rugged football player from Murray State University in Kentucky. But he seemed to be injury-prone. When he was right, though, the 6-foot 3-inch Mains could throw his 250 pounds around with a great deal of authority.

Alex Karras, the cherubic-looking practical joker from Iowa, was easily the standout of the starting unit. He was also the smallest, stretching out to a mere 6 feet 2 inches and weighing 245 pounds.

The Lions of 1959 were a sluggish ballclub, as their record of three wins, eight losses, and one tie indicated, which left them in fifth place in the six-team Western Division. But the point statistics showed what was really wrong with the Lions—lack of scoring punch.

Offensively, they scored 203 points during the twelve-game season, or an average of slightly less than 17 points per game. That was second lowest in the entire NFL; only Washington, in the Eastern Division, racked up fewer points. Defensively,

Detroit was somewhat better. The team yielded 275 points, or just under 23 points per game. That was a better average than four other NFL teams.

Thus there was room for improvement everywhere, and it was the defense that grew stronger.

In 1960, Gil Mains lost his starting job for two very good reasons. First, he suffered a leg injury and couldn't seem to regain his old form. But, even in his best days, Mains couldn't have held on to the job because of the second reason—a 6-foot 5-inch rookie from Maryland State College. His name was Roger Brown.

Detroit got off on the wrong foot as the 1960 season opened. There was some unhappiness over personalities on the team and a lot of growling and muttering; it looked like 1959 all over again. Then, after one tough loss, Alex Karras stomped into the locker room and roared, "From now on I'm gonna start acting like a man!"

With a measure of harmony restored, the Lions promptly ripped off seven victories in the next nine games, finishing second in their division, a climb of three notches. First downs for the opposition were less frequent and the offense held up better, all of which showed up in the scoring statistics: Lions, 239 points; opposition, 212. The defense had allowed an average of five points less per game than the previous year, and the offense had scored three points more.

There were many people who said flatly that Roger Brown was worth eight points, that he had made the difference.

In 1961, the NFL adopted a fourteen-game schedule, and once more Detroit finished second, a bare half-game ahead of the Baltimore Colts. And, although the Lions probably couldn't have taken the championship away from Green Bay, a couple of their losses were real heartbreakers.

Against Baltimore, Karras put the big rush on Johnny Unitas and deflected a pass just as it left Johnny U's hand. The ball wobbled into the air and was grabbed by Baltimore's running back Joe Perry, who sped off for twenty-five yards. The Colts won, 17–14, on that play.

They blew a 20–17 lead over San Francisco in the last seven seconds of play, when a field goal tied the score.

The last game of the season, against the Philadelphia Eagles, was particularly galling. The Eagles had beaten the Lions during the exhibition season, and Detroit was out to get even. It looked as if they had the game, too, as they kept stopping the Eagles' running back, Clarence Peaks, time and again. Once Peaks couldn't pick up less than a yard on the fourth down!

The Lions took a 24–17 lead into the last few minutes, and when Sonny Jurgensen engineered a drive to the 13-yard line, the Detroit front four dug in again. Peaks tried an end sweep and was hit for a 9-yard loss. The Eagles lined up for a field goal. But it was a fake, and it worked. The pass caught Detroit's secondary out of position, the touchdown was made, and the successful try for the point tied the game. Later the Eagles won it on a field goal.

In the Playoff Bowl, the Lions unleashed all their frustrations on their tormentors, the Eagles. Detroit practically ran them out of the ball park. Karras, Brown, and company seemed to be in the Philly huddle as they anticipated plays and kept belting the passer. The first time the sub quarterback King Hill tried to run a play, Brown stormed in and creamed him before the befuddled passer had time to look up. On almost every sequence of plays it seemed as if the Eagles were faced with a third-and-9 situation. The final score, 38–10, didn't tell the whole story. It was a massacre.

The 8–5–1 finish in 1961 seemed to indicate that Detroit might reach the top if the club could get some offensive power. But to get strength, it had to give up strength. The Lions' strongest area was their front four. Detroit gambled and broke off a piece of it.

Before the start of the 1962 season, Detroit and Cleveland completed a three-for-three trade. The Lions acquired the quarterback Milt Plum, the running back Tom Watkins, and Dave Lloyd, linebacker, in exchange for Jim Ninowski, quarterback; Hopalong Cassady, halfback, and Bill Glass, defensive end. And then, determined to live dangerously, Detroit swapped with Washington for another ball carrier, giving up Steve Junker, who was listed as a possible replacement for Glass. So who was left to man the first line of defense?

Standing in the wings was Sam Williams, 6 feet 5 inches and weighing 235 pounds. Williams had gone to Los Angeles from Michigan State University, but the Rams wanted Jim Davis, a defensive halfback of the Lions, to become one of their coaches. They had given Williams to Detroit a couple of years previously. Most of the time Williams had alternated between the offensive and defensive lines. He was a spot player at best, or so everyone thought. Still, the end position was his if he could take it from one of the rookies in camp. And he sure did!

Yet no one thought he could become another Bill Glass. Why, then, did Detroit take such risks, breaking up one of the best front fours in pro football? The answer was obvious; it was thought that with Brown and Karras up front, the rest of the line would have an easier time. They were already widely regarded as the best pair of tackles in the league.

In a football uniform, doing the job he was paid to do, Alex Karras was pure destruction on legs. But off the field he was a grinning, near-sighted, fun-loving, full-fledged comedian. He told the wildest, most impossible stories, all with a straight face. For instance, it was a fact that "in another life" he had been an aide to George Washington. Also, he had been the right-hand man to Adolf Hitler and Hermann Goering (whom he called "Bavarian Fats"); and it was well known to one and all that Hitler's girl friend, Eva Braun, was really his sister. Small wonder that one sportswriter called him "a regular Jackie Gleason with cleats."

Alex's father had been a doctor of a kind almost extinct today. He treated the rich and poor alike, and when he died everyone owed him money (mostly uncollectible). Mrs. Karras went back to work as a nurse, while Alex sold papers and worked in the Gary, Indiana, steel mills banking furnaces and at everything else he could put his hand to.

He really didn't want to play high school football, but two of his brothers were on the team (both later went on to play pro football with NFL teams) and there was no way he could get out of it. So the unwilling future star made all-state in three years of varsity play.

Karras really studied the game of football and found ways to stay healthy even against the toughest opponents. He shortened his running stride so his knees would be close together when he was hit. He shortened his cleats so they wouldn't stick in the turf. And even in pro ball, he never had too much difficulty with his knees, whereas torn cartilages and assorted knee problems are a common occupational hazard with most other players.

After a fine career at the University of Iowa, Karras found himself with the Lions, but he impressed absolutely nobody. In part it was his own fault, because he was lazy. Also, he spent so much time acting as chauffeur to Bobby Layne that he sometimes forgot all about playing football.

And surprisingly, Karras was the nervous type. Before a game he would get so keyed up that he became physically ill.

The man playing alongside him, Roger Brown, was somewhat different in style and temperament. Brown seldom got excited before a game, but once the contest started, he had a single-track mind: grab the guy with the football and heave him into the grandstand!

As a kid in Nyack, New York, Brown had two great loves—music and junk. He would scavenge through junkyards, looking for old bicycle parts and anything else he thought "valuable." He worked his way through Maryland State College as a disk jockey for a local radio station. Roger just liked to keep busy and play records—and a little football on the side.

As a freshman, Brown was a pile-driving fullback, scattering tacklers like a high wind gusting through a stack of straw. And in spite of his bulk, he was surprisingly fast. In 1960, when he was named to the All-Star college squad, Brown engaged in a series of fifty-yard dashes against the rest of the budding pros. He was beaten just twice, by two running backs!

Brown didn't last long as a Maryland State fullback. He was just too big and strong to be wasted back there, carrying the ball. The coach shoved him into the line, and he became one of the best in the country. The Lions picked him in the fourth round of the annual draft. He was an "extra" choice, part payment from the Pittsburgh Steelers, who had acquired the rights to Bobby Layne from the Lions.

Big Roger was a regular from the moment he strapped on his helmet. In the first exhibition game, against the Cleveland Browns, he intercepted a pass and galloped twenty-three yards for a touchdown. Along the way, four Cleveland tacklers jumped on his back and attempted to wrestle him down, but Brown carried them over the goal line like sacks of flour.

Brown learned quickly, especially the proper way to use his hands. In his case it was the delivery of a hard slap over the helmet of the opposing lineman. Later in his career, in a pro bowl game, he belted an offensive lineman, Vince Promuto of the Washington Redskins, three times, and with such force that Promuto couldn't hear the signals! Moreover, what he did was absolutely legal.

So the Lions went into the 1962 season with high hopes that this would be the year of their return to glory. And for a time it looked as if they were on their way, as they peeled off three victories in a row. Then they ran into the Green Bay Packers.

Detroit was really up for the game, and the Pack didn't do too well. Time and again the front four made Bart Starr get rid of the ball when he didn't want to, as they put on a rush that scattered the Green Bay offensive line all over the turf. The Lions scored a touchdown and added the point; the best

Green Bay could manage was a pair of field goals. The game went into its last moments with the Lions ahead, 7–6.

It looked like a sure win. The Lions had the ball. All they had to do was keep it on the ground, run a few plays, and if they made a first down, fine; if not, they could punt out, and with Yale Lary kicking, the Packers would find themselves deep in their own territory, too far away to affect the outcome.

Perhaps Milt Plum figured that Green Bay would be caught napping if he tried a pass. If Terry Barr could slip behind the in-tight Packer defense, he might grab the long bomb and put the game out of reach. There could be no other reason for such a call. But the strategy backfired. Barr slipped and fell, the ball was intercepted, and Green Bay came back to score another field goal. The Lions lost, 9–7.

After the game, Karras was in a murderous mood. He tore into the locker room, flung his helmet at Plum and was ready to clobber the man he called "a blue-eyed sissy milk-drinker." Fortunately, teammates separated the two, and Plum escaped with his life.

The next loss was to the New York Giants. At first it looked as if the score would have to be totaled by computers, as each team hit pay dirt the first time it had possession of the football. Plum tossed a 48-yard scoring strike to Gail Cogdill, and the Giants came back with a drive of their own, led by Y.A. Tittle. The bald-headed New York passer outfoxed the Detroit foursome and the secondary as well with his fakes and feeds and soft screen passes.

Then the game settled down into its expected defensive struggle, as Robustelli, Katcavage, Grier, and Modzelewski, the outstanding New York front four, and the Detroit forward wall traded punch for punch. The Lions scored again on a four-yard plunge by Tom Watkins; but a blocked kick, a couple of penalties, and Title's screen passes—it was like lobbing hand grenades and destroying any possible defense—won the touchdown back for the Giants.

But the Lions were beaten again, and it was an interception that did it. One of Plum's throws was picked off, New York converted it into a field goal, and the final score was 17–14, Giants. It was a tough one to lose. The New York running attack had been held to just sixty-seven yards!

But the season wasn't over yet, and the Detroit front four became the terror of the NFL. Sammy Williams was a pleasant surprise, blossoming into a first-rate defensive end. Darris McCord was his usual ready-steady self. Brown and Karras were just unbelievable.

In one sequence against Los Angeles, Roman Gabriel came into the game at quarterback with a normal first-and-10 situation. When he left a few seconds later, it was third-and-31!

In the Chicago Bears game, sportswriters covered their eyes and shook their heads because they couldn't believe what they were seeing. The Bears' quarterback, Billy Wade, had dropped back into his end zone to pass. Protecting him was Ted Karras, Alex's brother. Spectators swear that Brown picked up the 243-pound Teddy Karras and *threw him at Wade!* Brown later shrugged and said he'd just given his teammates' brother "a good, hard shove." Regardless of which version was correct, the blocking Karras went flying through the air, hit Wade, and both went down in a heap for a 2-point safety.

With that kind of defensive play, the Lions rolled along into second place, two games behind the Green Bay Packers. But there was still a chance to catch up, or at least eat into the lead. For there was a Thanksgiving Day clash scheduled between the Lions and the Pack. Furthermore, it was to be televised nationally.

Green Bay came into Tiger Stadium undefeated. The Packers had reeled off ten victories in a row—twelve if the last two of the previous season were counted. Vince Lombardi's squad was undoubtedly the best-drilled, most solid gang of football players to be found in any league, at any time. It had a marvelous defensive unit, and a dandy offense, headed by Bart Starr at quarterback, with such receivers as Max McGee, Boyd Dowler, and Ron Kramer. Carrying the mail were Paul Hornung, Tom Moore, and hard-nose Jim Taylor. Nobody made merry with this ballclub. Nobody, that is, until the Detroit Lions got through stomping them on Thanksgiving Day of 1962. Everybody who saw that game—and that includes millions of turkey-stuffed fans sitting in front of their television sets—wholeheartedly agreed that it was the greatest exhibition of defensive football since the sport was invented.

Green Bay kicked off, and the Lions started driving in a hurry. They reached the Packer 32, when a fumble cost them possession, the Packers recovering on their own 17-yard line.

Starr started to move the Pack, and a fast pass to Max McGee ate up 26 yards. Jim Taylor picked up 4 yards at left end. All very nice. A ball-control game; quite typical of Green Bay's offense. Little did the Packers know what was in store for them!

On the next play, Karras broke through and dropped Tom Moore for a loss of 3 yards. Then Darris McCord and Karras, aided and abetted by Joe Schmidt, a linebacker, crashed in and nailed Starr before he could throw the football. A delay-of-game penalty didn't help the Packers either. Now they were back on their own 39.

Starr dropped to pass. When he looked up, there was an evil-looking monster named Roger Brown coming in to destroy him. Starr ran for his life, but it did no good. Brown caught him 15 yards behind the line of scrimmage and pounded him into the turf.

Stunned by the savagery of the defense, the usually reliable Boyd Dowler got off a wobbly kick that went out on the Green Bay 39. Recognizing a break when they saw one, the Lions struck swiftly. Lewis gained 3 yards at left tackle, Nick Pietrosante added 3 more on a draw play. With Green Bay in close to shut off the first-down attempt, Plum went to the air, completing a 33-yard heave to Gail Cogdill. Wayne Walker converted. Score: Detroit 7, Green Bay 0.

Back came the Packers. In two plays Tom Moore picked up 18 yards, and it looked as if the Pack were rolling. Then a whole pride of Lions stormed in and nailed Starr for a 9-yard loss. On the next play the Lions forced Starr out of the pocket with their rush. The game Green Bay quarterback fled toward the sidelines and managed to pick up 5 yards. When Jim Taylor tried to buck up the middle, Sammy Williams was there to close the hole and knock down the ball carrier for a 1-yard loss.

Back to punt, Boyd Dowler was rushed again, the kick partly blocked. The ball rolled dead on the Detroit 44. But before the Lions could start moving, a fumble gave the ball back to Green Bay. Still, it seemed as if Lombardi's boys were bent on self-destruction, because Tom Moore promptly fumbled the ball back to the Lions.

This time they didn't let the break go to waste. They pushed and shoved, and Plum's 27-yard toss to Cogdill was the touchdown play. Walker again added the point. Now it was 14–0.

What followed was a nightmare for Green Bay, the likes of which had not been seen in pro football for years—if at all!

Herb Adderley took the kickoff 6 yards in his own end zone and carried it out to the 21. Starr's first passing attempt was batted down at the line of scrimmage. On the next play, as Starr went back to pass again, he saw his nemesis, a dragon named Roger Brown, chasing him back, back, back. It was a bad dream, it couldn't be—but there he was. Brown caught Starr on the 6-yard line and dropped him with a thundering crash. The ball popped loose. Brown's buddy, Sammy Williams, was right there to pick it up and skip merrily into the end zone. The extra point made the score 21–0.

By now the Pack was thoroughly demoralized. Wasn't there any force on planet Earth to stop that crazy man, Roger Brown? Evidently not. Because, with the ensuing kickoff out of the way, the big buster from Nyack started all over again. First, Brown tore in and smeared Jim Taylor for a loss of 6 yards. Tom Moore got 3 yards back with a line plunge. Starr went back to pass again, and . . . oh, no! Not you again, Roger Brown! Starr was driven back across his own goal line and bounced down with tooth-rattling force. Two points for the Lions.

The carnage continued the next time Green Bay obtained possession. By this time the Lion linebackers decided that it wasn't fair for the front four to have all the fun, so they got some of the easy pickings too.

When Starr tried to pass on first down, he kept a sharp eye out for Roger Brown. But Starr was looking the wrong way, because Wayne Walker sliced in and nailed him for a 9-yard loss. Determined to complete at least one more pass before he was killed, Starr did manage to hit Dowler for 13 yards. But on the next play, into the line, Jim Taylor lost 2 yards. It was absolutely amazing how they were stopping the Green Bay fullback. There was no question in anyone's mind that he was the second-best fullback in football, only Jimmy Brown of Cleveland topping him.

The Packers fooled around a bit more on the sequence, but it didn't amount to much. Max McGee, punting in place of Dowler, kept the ball and turned right end for a first down. But after that, Green Bay played the same old tune. Taylor hit left tackle for no gain. Then, while Starr kept his eye peeled for Brown, Darris McCord came in to dump the Pack passer for a loss of 9. In desperation, Starr managed to connect with Ron Kramer for 19 yards, just 36 inches short of the first down.

With a fourth-and-1 situation on the Detroit 37, Green Bay elected to go for it instead of trying a long field goal. Starr went by the book. He fed the ball to Jim Taylor. Big Jim tried to go over right guard, but he was stacked up at the line of scrimmage and Detroit took over on downs.

The Lions didn't go anywhere, and Green Bay got the ball

back. By then Alex Karras was beginning to feel like a stepchild, for he hadn't sat on Bart Starr for some time.

On the first play of the sequence, Karras thrust aside everyone not in a Lion jersey and slapped down the passer for a 9-yard loss. Starr's next pass, intended for McGee, dropped harmlessly to the ground. Then Karras broke in again and slammed Starr for a 6-yard loss. So, three passing attempts resulted in *minus* 15 yards for the Packers.

But Green Bay retained possession on a roughing-the-kicker penalty. Whereupon Bart Starr, always one of the best in the business, threw five completions in a row for 56 yards!

Trying to get on the scoreboard before the halftime gun sounded, Green Bay tried a field goal from the 31. But it was blocked—by Roger Brown, who had been taking it easy since his heroics earlier in the period. The half ended with Detroit leading, 23–0.

In all probability, during the intermission Vince Lombardi gave his charges a tongue-lashing, especially his offensive linemen. Whatever he said, it didn't work, because Green Bay's attack fizzled out two plays after the kickoff. After Moore got a couple of yards through left tackle, Starr's pass was intercepted by Night Train Lane. The interception cost the Pack dearly, for the Lions moved close enough to score another field goal.

Again the Packers tried mightily, but it was useless. Tom Moore, trying left guard, was stacked up. Joe Schmidt filtered through on a blitz and bounced the bruised Starr for a 15-yard loss.

Things were no better for Green Bay the next time it got the ball. Tom Moore ran into Karras, and the result was a loss of 2. Trying to escape from another Lion blitz, Starr ran and hid, but picked up 5 yards on the play. He wasn't so fortunate on the next call. Everybody on the Detroit team crashed in and spilled the battered Packer passer for a loss of 10.

It wasn't until early in the fourth period that Green Bay

scored, and then it wasn't through offensive efforts. Bill Quinlan picked off one of Milt Plum's passes and scooted 28 yards into the end zone. Although he fumbled, Willie Davis was there to recover for the touchdown.

But by then everyone knew that the Packers were a thoroughly beaten ballclub. The game flickered away, with only two incidents worth noting:

Once more, Roger Brown dropped Bart Starr behind the line of scrimmage. It was a 5-yard loss.

And Jim Taylor, almost weeping with frustration, bulled his way to a touchdown from 4 yards out.

The final score was Detroit 26, Green Bay 14.

The game's statistics were a joy to all who love defensive football. Green Bay's vaunted rushing attack, with all its built-in ball-control gimmicks, netted exactly seventy-three yards. The totals showed that Bart Starr had lost eighty-three yards attempting to pass. The Detroit front four had risen to the occasion magnificently.

For the play-by-play story of that historic contest and, incidentally, a sample of how the NFL keeps its game records see page 135.

The Packers recovered from that debacle. It was the only game they lost all year, and they went on to break up the Giants in the championship game, retaining their title as masters of pro football.

Detroit lost one more game, and finished with an 11–3–0 record, two games ahead of the Chicago Bears. The Lions were also second in defense (Green Bay was first), allowing just 177 points over the season. It seemed that with a little more guile at the trading post, or a bit more luck with draft choices, the Lions might take it all the following season. Look at that fantastic front four!

But it was not to be. Unwittingly and unwillingly, Alex Karras throttled all such plans. For the all-pro tackle was called on the carpet for gambling. Nobody ever accused him of trying to throw a game, or shaving points, or anything else dishonest. But Commissioner Pete Rozelle had a blanket rule—no gambling with bookies by football players. And he was right about that. Paul Hornung of the Packers was also charged with the same offense.

Both players sat out the 1963 season. And both teams paid the price. Green Bay finished second to Chicago, while Detroit slid to fourth. Never again did the Lions and their marvelous foursome regain their supremacy. Even after Karras came back the following year, Detroit was fourth again. Then, one by one, the front four broke up, by trade or retirement.

But, for one supreme moment, on Thanksgiving Day of 1962, the pride of Detroit Lions had the greatest defensive team and the greatest front four in all of pro football!

The Doomsday Defense

IT WAS UNDER TOM LANDRY'S DIRECTION that the New York Giants (and thus professional football in general) developed and perfected the 4–3 defense, utilizing four men up front and three linebackers. It was as startling an innovation as any in football, and proved conclusively that Landry was an inventive man, a student of the game.

Landry had the material to work with, and that made his job easier. He was attempting only what was possible; had he attempted the impossible, it would have taken him somewhat longer. Strangely, he did try the impossible, and because he did not have the material at the outset, it took him six years to accomplish it.

What he tried to do was create an attack that would overcome his own brainchild—the 4–3. To some extent he succeeded. At least he forced the formation to become more sophisticated, to use a combination of zone defense, man-to-man, free safety and weak safety alignments, and other forms of multiple defense. Because he was continually tinkering around, he became one of the inventors of the multiple offense.

Like most inventions, necessity was the mother; and in Landry's case, poverty was the father. When he took control of the Dallas Cowboys in 1960, all he had was opportunity, because he certainly didn't have much in the way of talented personnel.

The Dallas Cowboys were formed in something of a hurry, so fast, in fact, that they never did have a chance to get in on the draft selections. The club was hastily stocked with a motley crew including the expendables from other clubs, a few outright rejects, free agents who managed to hook on somehow, minor-league hopefuls, and others. No fewer than 193 players of various talent passed through the Dallas training camp, including a milkman! Those who remained marched proudly out to do battle with the combat units of seasoned NFL teams. They never had a chance!

Landry settled on Eddie LeBaron as his quarterback. LeBaron was a good one, with a strong arm and the brains to handle a team. He had played a lot of good football; in fact he lasted eleven years in the league, four of them with the Cowboys. But Eddie was too small to be great. When the big defensive men came bearing in on him, he couldn't locate his downfield receivers.

Backing up LeBaron was "Dandy" Don Meredith, a rookie out of Southern Methodist University. There were a few other serviceable players scattered through the lineup, some of whom would improve with experience. But this wasn't to be the year of the Cowboy.

Since Landry had practically invented pro football defenses, it followed that he knew a good deal about offense. And he was also a shrewd evaluator of players. Almost immediately he realized that it would probably be easier for his boys to score than prevent the other team from scoring. He began to experiment with various subtle changes in the T—he later would come up with the I formation—and tried desperately to teach the moves to his players. Meredith once explained his skipper's technique:

"Landry would be at the blackboard, saying, 'Okay, we'll do this, and then they'll do that, and then we'll do this . . .' And I'd say, 'Coach, what if they don't do that?' And Landry would say, 'But they *will* do that.' And sure enough, on Sunday, that's just what they'd do!"

When Landry was hired, he said that it would take him five years to produce a respectable team. Because he had missed the player draft—while the other expansion teams had their crack at the top college players when they started—it took him six years, even then the Cowboys managed to get only a 50–50 split on the season. Before that their record looked like the statistics of a disaster area. In 1960, it was 0–11–1, and then it was 4–9–1, 5–8–1, 4–10–0, and 5–8–1.

The club as a whole kept improving, but the antics of some of the players could have been enough to drive a lesser man into an early grave. One of Landry's biggest headaches was Don Meredith, who sometimes displayed all the ability of a sandlot teenager, and at others looked like the best quarterback in pro football. In 1965, for example, Meredith came up with a sore arm early in the year, so Landry turned loose his two prize substitutes, Jerry Rhome and Craig Morton. Neither could get the team rolling, and pretty soon Meredith discovered that his arm was sound again. So Landry let him play against Pittsburgh, and what he saw almost reduced him to tears. Dandy Don was intercepted, he dropped the snap from center on a field goal attempt, and he also dropped the ball on the Pittsburgh 10-yard line when he seemed headed for a sure touchdown with nobody within yards of him.

Then Meredith led the Cowboys to five victories in their next seven games!

Landry hadn't neglected defense completely; he just didn't have the men to do a proper job and had to wait until the right players showed up before the defense could do a respectable job. Some of his linemen weren't bad, but there wasn't an authentic star among them. When the good ones did arrive, it took a long time before everything fell into place.

Bob Lilly turned up in 1961. Lilly's coach at Texas Christian University said that he was the best tackle he had ever coached. Lilly had the quickness of a young puma and eye-blinking strength to match. At TCU he had made something of a name for himself by singlehandedly lifting a Volkswagen out of the street and placing it on the sidewalk!

There were two things wrong with his debut in pro football. First, he appeared to be lazy—he wasn't putting out, or didn't seem to. Perhaps that was because of the second reason: Lilly had played tackle, and Landry installed him at defensive end. The 6-foot 5-inch 255-pounder seemed lost there. He kept worrying about the pass rush, and sealing off the end sweeps, and whether or not the linebackers would move up fast enough to give him a hand. The future all-pro was no ball of fire his first year, nor his second. Midway through 1963, Landry decided to switch him to tackle, where he could be free to roam and break through, concentrating strictly on the pass rush and closing up the middle on power plays. Lily didn't become an overnight sensation, but he did begin a remarkable improvement.

George Andrie was a find out of Marquette University. Andrie didn't get to play football during his senior year because Marquette had dropped the sport as a major athletic event. Rather than transfer to another school and perhaps lose some of his college credits, Andrie sat out the year. But he had the potential, and Landry stuck with him. Andrie was big—6 feet 7 inches tall and 255 pounds. He moved well to the outside. He was a natural defensive end.

The Cowboys traded for Jim Colvin, who had been a regular with Baltimore. Few football players were as gutsy as Colvin, as willing to play while hurting. It was almost as though the fates were testing him. As a seventh grader, he couldn't play peewee football because he was too small. In the eighth grade a blood disorder prevented him from playing. As a sophomore at Orange High School in Texas, he tore a leg muscle. As a senior he broke a bone in his foot but played anyway with a special brace. But he kept coming and growing, and by the time he had left the University of Houston he was a 6-foot 2-inch, 250-pound bundle of muscular grit.

By 1964 the Dallas defensive record looked pretty good, even though its won-lost average didn't. For the first time the Cowboys yielded fewer than 300 points over a season. In their sometimes good-sometimes bad showings, they grabbed the quarterback a total of forty-five times, which equaled Green Bay's efforts. However, they also allowed ten passing touchdowns that covered thirty yards or more, and that wasn't so good. The combat line, which included Lilly, Andrie, Colvin, and Maury Youmans, was beginning to shape up.

In 1965, Dallas fans began asking "What's a Jethro Pugh?" And even after he'd been in action for a while they kept asking the same question. Because Pugh wasn't particularly well known. His alma mater, Elizabeth City State College in North Carolina, had an enrollment of perhaps a thousand students. The Cowboys chose him eleventh in the draft, with an eye toward turning the 6-foot 6-inch 250-pounder into an offensive tackle. In his rookie year, Pugh played mostly on specialty teams, and his hustle stamped him as a comer. After he blocked a field goal against the Giants, he began entering the game on all field-goal attempts and sure passing down, when his fast rush would come in handy.

Finally, there was Willie Townes, a 6-foot 5-inch, 265-pound broth of a boy. There was only one problem as far as Willie was concerned—he liked the groceries too much. Willie had a tendency to balloon up to awesome proportions, and when he first reported to Dallas, Landry fined him $50 for every overweight pound. Landry had insisted that he report weighing 270; Willie came in at 282, but Landry forgave two of the twelve extra pounds and made it an even $500 fine. At those prices, Willie decided he could do without the mashed potatoes and gravy. After a diet of orange juice and vitamin pills, he dropped to 265, and since he felt better and moved quicker at that weight, there he remained.

Townes was a rookie in 1966. So was Ernie Stautner—as a line coach. Stautner, an all-time, all-pro lineman, knew that the basic ingredients for a great line were there. All he had to do was set fire to the players somehow. He began to instill in them the idea that life in the pit could be fun. "Just hit them," he would plead. "Hit them and hit them again. Pretty soon you'll start enjoying hitting the other guy. You'll be looking forward to it."

The year of the great transformation was 1966. Landry was never a great one for popping off, but he recognized that this was a potentially great Dallas team, especially on defense. Very quietly he let it be known that his boys might go all the way if they got a few good breaks and stayed healthy.

As if to insure that the whole world heard their skipper, the Cowboys practically destroyed the New York Giants in the season's opener, 52–7. The line let New York know who was boss from the opening series, when George Andrie banged down Earl Morrall for losses of 5 yards and then 7 yards. New York got rid of the ball in a hurry, Dallas marched 70 yards in fourteen plays and had a score.

In the next Giant series, Morrall began running for his life. The Dallas rush was so hard on one play that Morrall just got rid of the ball anywhere at all, and it was almost caught by the Giant coach, Allie Sherman, near the New York bench.

After Dallas had rolled up the score so that New York couldn't come back even if they played a doubleheader, the Cowboys eased up. After all, it was only the first game; why get so excited?

A real test for the Cowboys came in the Minnesota game. The Vikings were tough enough, but that wasn't what gave the opposition fits. Every man in the line would feel like limp spaghetti after an afternoon spent chasing the scrambling Fran Tarkenton all over the turf. One Tarkenton scramble actually consumed a full sixteen seconds—and that's a long time in football. He dropped back, ran right, reversed his field and ran left, then backward a few yards, then to his left again, finally threw the pass—and completed it! When a pursuing 250-pound lineman keeps running and stopping and changing directions for sixteen seconds, he generally needs at least as much time to recover his wind. Yet Lilly knocked down three passes, and the Cowboys caught up with Tarkenton three times. Dallas won, 28–17.

Then the Cowboys beat the Atlanta Falcons and the Eagles; the Philadelphia game was really no contest. And it was then that Dallas made it clear that nobody could run against their line. They yielded a total of thirty-eight yards on the ground and didn't permit the Eagles to score until the last seven minutes of the game. By that time who cared? The final score was 56–7.

It was in the disappointing 10–10 tie with St. Louis that the Cowboys established their reputation for being tough cookies when their backs were to the wall. In the second period, for example, it took the Cardinals six plays to score from in close. Three shots into the middle from the 1-yard line didn't do it; a soft pass into the corner of the end zone did.

In the third quarter, St. Louis had the ball, first-and-10 from the Dallas 13. Two plays gained 6. On third down, Jethro Pugh muscled in, chased Charley Johnson, and dropped him for a 23-yard loss. A subsequent field-goal attempt missed.

In the fourth quarter, on third-and-1, Johnson tried to sneak for the yard and didn't make it. The ball was on the 20, but instead of going for the yard again, and perhaps missing, Johnson decided it would be smarter to take the field goal.

They began calling the Dallas line "The Doomsday Defense." In the shadow of its own goalposts, the line became a fortress, a row of tank traps, an impenetrable wall. Running against it in short yardage situations was futile. Only the top backs in the league could get through, and even then it was a sometimes thing.

The Cowboys lost to Cleveland, 30–21, but by the statistics you would never know it. The Cleveland passer completed nine for twenty-one while Meredith hit twenty-six for forty-five! Dallas gained 413 yards net to 264 for the Browns. The Cowboys knocked down passes before they crossed the scrimmage line, and they stopped runners. But in the crucial situations Cleveland capitalized on the breaks and Dallas didn't. Besides, Cleveland sacked Meredith five times for thirty-one yards, while the Cowboys didn't drop the Cleveland quarterback at all. There was a lesson to be learned, and it wasn't lost on the Doomsday Defense. A batted-down pass is great, but it's just another incompleted pass, no loss and no gain. Dumping the quarterback before he can throw is a loss of yardage, and every little bit helps.

Dallas beat Pittsburgh, 52–21, but those three touchdowns weren't the fault of the Dallas front four. An intercepted pass put the Cowboys behind at the outset, and when they later moved ahead of the Steelers a 93-yard kickoff return put another touchdown on the board for Pittsburgh. The third Steeler score was also the result of a pass interception. Pittsburgh took over on the Dallas 9, but it still took four plays to punch into the end zone.

The 24–23 upset by the Philadelphia Eagles wasn't the fault of the front four either. Blame the special teams, and the ability of Timmy Brown to run like the devil when he got the ball. Dallas scored first, recovering a fumble by Earl Grós (Willie Townes pounced on it). Tim Brown responded by running the kickoff back 93 yards for a touchdown.

Dallas moved ahead, first 10–7 and then 17–7. So Tim Brown took another kickoff and went all the way again, this time a mere 90 yards. And after a 67-yard runback of a punt, the Eagles led 21–17.

That broke the Cowboy's spirit. No sooner would they score than the other club pulled some fancy run and won it all back—and more. The Dallas defense dropped Norm Snead five times, and he lost 33 yards in the process. The Philadelphia average was 3.2 yards per play. Snead completed only five of seventeen tries. But they don't pay off on statistics, only what the scoreboard shows.

As any sports fan will agree, no contest is more thrilling than a football game in which a team comes from behind and then the lead starts changing hands. The Dallas front four took a back seat as Washington's Sonny Jurgensen and Dandy Don Meredith took turns thrilling the spectators. Dallas was ahead, 21–6, when Jurgensen and his Redskins went on the warpath. A 4-yard scoring pass and one good for 78 yards and a touchdown, plus a field goal, put the Skin ahead, 23–21. Dallas came back with a touchdown, only to have Jurgensen connect with his scatback, Charley Taylor, for another touchdown. Dandy Don was faced with an almost impossible task; his club trailed, 30–28, the ball was on his own 3-yard line, and all the time outs had been used up. But he passed and he handed off and he commanded his troops like a general, and with 15 seconds left, Danny Villanueva booted a field goal from the 20!

Next it was Pittsburgh again, a much tougher version of the team the Cowboys had massacred earlier in the season. The aroused Steelers threatened to tear the Cowboys loose from their helmets. Lilly, Andrie, and the others had to reach the heights to stop them, and they did. The Doomsday Defense put on a show near the end of the first half that had the Steelers dizzy.

Dallas had missed a field-goal attempt, and it's 7–0 lead looked shaky as Pitt went to the air to try for a tie. On the first play the entire front four fired in. The Pittsburgh passer was hit as he threw, and the pass fell incomplete. Then Bob Lilly roared up and dropped him for a loss of 5. On the next play it was Lilly again, throwing the quarterback, Ron Smith, for a loss of 7. The half ended with Dallas still leading.

The Dallas shock troops enjoyed their finest hour against Pittsburgh. When the statisticians had finished their work they found that the Cowboy line had flattened the Steelers' passer twelve times—a league record—for a combined loss of 77 yards. One rush that didn't get into the statistics involved Bob Lilly. The all-pro end bore down on Ron Smith like a runaway truck. Trying to avoid being killed, Smith just threw the ball away. The referee caught the infraction and penalized the Steelers 15 yards for intentionally grounding the ball. The passer was on his feet, but the loss was bigger than if he had been spilled. The final score was only 20–7, but the Cowboy line outshone the score.

In winning against Cleveland, the Doomsday Defense staged another great show. In the fourth quarter, with Dallas leading 19–14, Cleveland had the ball on the Cowboy 11. Frank Ryan went back to pass, saw nobody clear, and fled to the sidelines for a gain of 2. On second down, a Ryan pass was broken up by Cornell Green's diving leap. Then Lilly and Andrie converged on Ryan, knocking him flat for a loss of 4. On fourth down, with the Browns looking for a field goal, Mike Gaechter, a defensive back, tore in and blocked it. Mel Renfro recovered, and the Dallas Cowboys were temporarily out of the woods. Later, with 4 minutes left, the secondary broke up two passes. Then Willie Townes flipped Ryan for a loss of 7, and it was Townes again, flattening Ryan for a loss of 6.

The Cardinals didn't beat Dallas, but the weather almost did. Playing in the fog-shrouded Cotton Bowl in 100 percent humidity, the Cowboys puffed and panted and staggered to a 31–17 victory. It was a must game for both teams, with first place at stake, but the front four of Dallas came through again. Five times they rode through to beat down the passer.

The Doomsday Defense

Dallas lost the next to Washington as Charlie Gogolak booted a field goal in the final seconds of play. But Landry's boys wound things up in a blaze of glory, beating the Giants and dumping its passer nine more times while doing it.

It was a new record for the Doomsday Defense. In fourteen games they had reached the quarterback *sixty* times! It was this feat that gave Dallas the Eastern Division championship. At last Tom Landry had made good his boast to the Dallas fans. He had given them a title.

The National League title game against Green Bay in the Cotton Bowl was one of the most exciting contests ever played. Sportswriters still talk about it as an example of how a stadium of fans can set off reverberations like earthquake shock waves.

Green Bay scored the first time it had the ball, in spite of heroic work by Bob Lilly. On the fourth play of the series he batted down a pass, and right after that Lilly guessed that Bart Starr would try a swing pass to his fullback, Jim Taylor. He guessed right, and dropped the big Packer fullback for a loss of 3. But Starr found the range, and Elijah Pitts took a 17-yarder for the touchdown.

An instant later the Cowboys were two touchdowns down, as Mel Renfro fumbled after taking the kickoff; Jim Grabowski picked up the ball and raced 18 yards into the end zone.

The Packers had one of pro football's finest front fours, but they couldn't contain the enraged Cowboy march. With Don Meredith passing and Dan Reeves running, Dallas had a touchdown with 4:27 left in the period. Four minutes later came the equalizer, with Don Perkins going off right guard from the 23.

Then the game settled down to a war of attrition. Green Bay scored a touchdown in the second period, Dallas countered with a field goal. In the third period the act was repeated; touchdown Green Bay, field goal Dallas. And in the fourth quarter the Packers scored again on a Bart Starr pass.

It was Bob Lilly who made the big play then, busting through to block the conversion. The Pack led, 34–20, with 5.20 left in the game.

Don Meredith filled the air with buzz bombs when the Cowboys got the ball again, and one connected, a 68-yarder. Now it was 34–27. Still time to pull it out.

Bart Starr tried frantically to get some insurance points for Green Bay, but the fired-up Dallas defense pressured him unmercifully. Dave Edwards, a linebacker, blitzed in to grab him for a loss of 8, then another pass was deflected by Willie Townes. Lee Roy Jordan, the middle linebacker, blitzed through a hole opened by the tackles and grabbed Jim Taylor as he took a swing pass, dropping him for a loss of 7. Don Chandler got off a puny punt that went all of 16 yards. Dallas took over on its own 47, with 2:06 left.

Here the Packer defense rose up. Dallas had gotten the ball down to the Green Bay 2-yard line because of a pass interference penalty. An offside pushed the Cowboys to the 6. A Meredith short pass put them back on the 2. On fourth down, with 45 seconds still left on the clock, as the thousands in the Cotton Bowl went berserk, Meredith flipped one toward Bob Hayes in the end zone. A Green Bay linebacker, Dave Robinson, leaped up and intercepted. The ballgame was over.

It was certainly no disgrace to lose to the Packers, especially in a tough game. Green Bay went on to win the first Super Bowl, handling Kansas City in surprisingly easy fashion, which made the Dallas effort all the more outstanding. And Landry had a club that was liberally sprinkled with players who were still young, and now had the experience of a championship game under their belts.

Dallas repeated the following year. Its record—9–5–0—wasn't as good, but the Cowboys still allowed fewer points in 1967 than any other team in their division.

The preliminary playoff game matched Dallas with Cleveland for the Eastern Conference championship. The Dallas defense performed nobly, specially Bob Lilly, who played with a broken heart. Only five days before, his seven-week-old daughter had died. The previous night the thriving infant had been put to bed; in the morning she was unaccountably dead.

The biggest thorn in the Cowboys' side was Leroy Kelly, the Browns' back who was trying to make Cleveland fans forget about Jimmy Brown. The Dallas four couldn't always contain him, but on one occasion they slammed the door on him with such force that Kelly was unable to go across in two tries from the 1-yard line! Dallas scored early and often to put Cleveland away, 52–14.

So it was Green Bay against Dallas in a rematch. This game wasn't played in the pleasant confines of the Cotton Bowl; rather it was staged in that open-air meat locker called Wisconsin, where the thermometer wore an overcoat to withstand the temperature of *13 below zero!* But the cold was the only difference. All the thrills were the same as in the previous year.

As before, the Packers jumped out to a two-touchdown lead before the frozen-fingered Cowboys could find their footing on the treacherously icy turf. The fact that the score was close at the end of the half was a tribute to the defense, especially the big four. In the second period, Willie Townes streaked in and turned Bart Starr into an icicle. Starr fumbled, George Andrie recovered the ball and scored. Later, Willie Wood let a punt slither off his numbed fingers, and the Cowboys turned the fumble into a field goal.

If the Dallas defense was tough, the Green Bay line and linebackers were even more so. However, the Cowboys started to adjust to the frozen conditions of the field, which they had not been able to do before. As an added gimmick, Don Meredith cut a hole in his jersey; he put his hand next to his stomach between plays to restore some feeling back into his fingers.

Time and again the Cowboys threatened. They advanced to the Green Bay 13, but Meredith fumbled. Back they came again. A terrific rush by the front line tossed Starr for a loss of

16, and the Cowboys took possession soon afterward. But Villanueva missed a long field goal. At last the Cowboys put it together with a bomb, Meredith to Lance Rentzel, and they led for the first time, 17–14.

Charged up, Dallas kept the Green Bay power in check until the final 5 minutes. Then the Packers started their final drive of the day, with Bart Starr showing why his field generalship placed him in the forefront of all passers.

By passing short and alternating his receivers, Starr soon had a Green Bay first down on the Dallas 1-yard line. Andrie, Lillie, Townes, and Pugh planted themselves firmly in the ice and defied the Packers to score.

It was Donny Anderson, the $600,000 bonus beauty, cracking into the line and getting stacked up by the Doomsday Defense. Again it was Anderson cracking hard straight ahead and being stopped at the line. Now only 20 seconds remained. A field goal would tie the game. but then all the momentum would be with the Cowboys. They would have stopped the Packer charge from only a yard out, and they would take the kickoff in the sudden-death finish. The Packers couldn't risk it.

Starr called his own number. It was Jerry Kramer, the all-pro guard, taking on Jethro Pugh, whose hands were so frozen that later his condition was described as the equivalent of second-degree burns. Kramer fired in hard; he and Ken Bowman at center moved Pugh back. Willie Townes was down low and he began to shove his opponent back. But he wasn't there in time. Starr fell over the goal line. It was another Packer victory!

Tom Landry did not give Dallas a championship team in his decade as head coach during the 1960's. He came close, starting from scratch. His men played great football once they gained experience and learned what sound coaching can do for a club. His Doomsday Defense proved that.

The Fearsome Foursome

AS I'VE SAID BEFORE, FOR A LONG TIME THE eleven men on the defensive unit were the unsung heroes of professional football. Especially the linemen. It was possible for a cornerback or safety to grab a few headlines with a spectacular interception and long return of a pass, but the linemen seldom got a chance to pick one off and run it into the end zone. Sure, it happened—but how often? So the big men mumbled and grumbled and did the job they were paid to do.

The 1960's produced a quartet of front players who, in their own way, will be remembered as fondly and wistfully as the old Four Horsemen of Notre Dame. That would be the Fearsome Foursome of the Los Angeles Rams. Ask any knowledgeable football fan which front line in the National League has been the best, consistently, year in and year out, and it's an even bet he'll name the Ram line. Even if he's biased and strongly home-town oriented, he will still toss a respectful nod toward the Los Angeles front four as the best in the business. The quality of that line isn't a publicity buildup; it's real.

In a way, rating the Ram line so high might seem a bit peculiar. Some years they have poured their hearts out and wound up with a record that looked pretty bad. The 1965 season was one of those. The Rams ended dead last, winning four and losing ten. But nobody blamed the defensive line, because the final tally sheets showed they had done their work well enough. That year the defensive unit gave up 328 points, about 23 per game. The offense scored 269 points, just over 19 per game. Figure it out; if the offense had been able to reach down and come up with just one more touchdown a game—or a couple of field goals—the Rams would have been a winning club.

It wasn't always that way for Los Angeles. Once it had been a real threat. From 1950 through 1955, the Rams won the Western Conference title three times. They didn't have a losing percentage in the other three, finishing second, third, or fourth, and some of the games they lost were decided in the last minute or two. But that was in the dear dim days when the Rams were noted for offense. On the same team were the two best passers in the league, Bob Waterfield and Norm Van Brocklin. Catching their throws were Tom Fears and Crazy Legs Hirsch. Toting the mail were Glenn Davis, Dan Towler, Tank Younger, and some other very able-bodied runners. No enemy lead was completely safe against the constant threat of the bomb, or the breakaway run.

In a way the Rams' own success was against them. Because of their high finishes, they generally picked last or next-to-last in the draft. Many of the cream choices were gone by the time they selected. So, when their regulars wore out and retired, the scoring threat ebbed away. Their stars simply could not be replaced.

The Rams went through a succession of coaches, but none seemed to help. Fiery Sid Gillman took over from 1955 to 1959; his over-all record was 28–31–1. Next came Waterfield, once a

Los Angeles hero. His record as coach was even worse, 9–24–1, and he relinquished the helm in midseason. Harland Svare took over. Svare had been a great linebacker with the New York Giants, then became defensive coach of the Rams. And it was Svare who built the Fearsome Foursome.

First to arrive on the scene was Lamar Lundy, who came up in 1957 while Gillman was running the team. Lundy, a 6-foot 6-inch 250-pounder out of Purdue, was originally drafted as a defensive lineman, but injuries to key players turned him into a slotback and tight end. Normally, that can't be done because defensive linemen haven't the speed. Or, if they are fast, they can't cut quickly, fake on the run, or catch passes. But Lundy was a fine all-around athlete (baseball, football, and basketball letters in college) and an intelligent, perceptive man (honor student at Purdue). He caught passes and he blocked well, and when reinforcements arrived, he was able to return to defensive end. Durable, with a high threshhold of pain, Lundy played 103 games in a row, until the final game of the 1964 season. Foot trouble sidelined him in 1965, but the following year he was back in the top echelon of NFL defensive linemen. Though he was never picked as an all-pro, those who went up against him swore that Lundy was among the most underrated players in the league.

Next to don the Ram jersey was David "Deacon" Jones, and the Deak is a whole book all by himself. There are any number of experts who, looking back over his performances, say flatly that he is one of the two best defensive ends in the history of the NFL, the other being Gino Marchetti of the Baltimore Colts. Strangely enough, Jones was far down on the draft list. But that was because he had played for a small school, and in the early 1960's not many scouts were beating the bushes for talent. Today they know better. Gold is where you find it.

A product of the Eatonville, Florida, ghetto, Jones was a star at Hungerford High in nearby Orlando, where he earned letters in football, baseball, basketball, and track. Normally, half a hundred big schools would have been pounding on the door of his frame house waving scholarships. But it didn't happen. Some Negro colleges wanted him. For some reason that he cannot explain to this day, Jones picked Mississippi Vocational. He stayed there just one year before switching to South Carolina State.

It was at State that he picked up his nickname. He began the practice of leading pregame prayers, and one of his teammates began calling him the Deacon. Soon everyone else did, too. Jones liked that. "I'm just one of the Jones boys when they call me Dave Jones," he said. "But Deacon—now that's a name that stands out."

Jones stood out in football, but nobody seemed to take note. The Rams got him by accident. They were scouting a running back who was playing against South Carolina State, but the only athlete anybody could see was Deacon Jones, who seemed to be playing in the enemy backfield. He became the *14th*-round pick.

When the 6-foot 5-inch rookie reported to camp, he saw that the Rams already had two pretty good men at the defensive end position, in Lamar Lundy and Gene Brito. But Jones was fast and Jones was heavy. At 260 pounds he figured that the defensive tackle spot wasn't impossible. But Brito became seriously ill, and Jones went to end after all. And since then, neither serious injury nor flashy rookies have succeeded in nudging him out. Jones will quit when he feels that his playing days are over, not five seconds before.

In 1962, Merlin Olsen came along. An All-American from Utah State University, Olsen set a new pattern for defensive linemen in the salary department. He asked for a $50,000 bonus and he got it without a quiver, because he was that good. In those days that was a staggering sum for a potential front four player.

The assistant coaches took one look at Olsen's 6-foot 5-inch frame, layered over with 275 pounds of destruction, and began a private war over his body. The offensive line coach, Vic Lindskog, wanted him, and so did the defensive coach, Don Paul. The issue was temporarily settled when the two Indian-wrestled for him and Lindskog won. Olsen became an offensive guard.

He remained there for exactly three or four scrimmages. Olsen was trapped out on one play, blocked to the side, and hit in the throat with a forearm. He couldn't breathe. Goodbye offense, hello defense.

The comical chaps who comment on football players sometimes point out the big linemen as prime examples of large size and small brains. Maybe that's true of a handful of football players, but not of Merlin Olsen. He was Phi Beta Kappa with an A-minus average, and the combination of brains and brawn turned him into a first-class tackle. Not at first, naturally, because he was just a rookie making rookie's mistakes. For instance, sometimes a fake would freeze him momentarily and catch him out of position. That happened in the Dallas game. A fake run made him overreact, and the real play went right by him for the touchdown. But with each game the offense found it increasingly difficult to fool him, and pretty soon it wasn't bamboozling him at all.

Roosevelt Grier arrived from the New York Giants in 1963, in a trade that sent John Lovetere from the Rams. Grier had a weight problem, or so it seemed. The 6-foot 5-inch tackle was listed at 290 pounds, but more often than not he ballooned up past the 300-pound mark. But he was almost impossible to overpower, and his strength was awe-inspiring. Years later, the hulking Grier—and another outstanding athlete, Rafer Johnson—would pinion one Sirhan Sirhan between them and fend off an enraged mob that wanted only to get at Senator Robert F. Kennedy's assassin and tear him to pieces.

A couple of seasons later, Roger Brown came from the Lions. By that time Grier was a crippled man, hobbling around as best he could.

These men made up the Fearsome Foursome of the Los Angeles Rams. They did not achieve instant stardom as a unit. That took time and experience. First they had to learn how to work together.

For example, Jones and Olsen, playing side-by-side, sometimes got confused in the rush. They tried to work out a stunting pattern, whereby the tackle would move to the outside, allowing Jones to cut in around Olsen and storm up the middle. That would confuse the blockers on their assignments. But sometimes they confused themselves as they both jammed into the middle.

In spite of losing records, the Ram defensive line became the talk of the league. Life in "the pit," as the middle of the line was often called, was rough on people, and the Fearsome Foursome made it even tougher. Lundy played steady ball, Grier was a rock, Olsen was a punisher up the middle, and Deacon Jones—well, his speed and strength made his name almost a dirty word to passers and running backs.

In one game he overtook Marv Woodson, one of the NFL's fastest halfbacks, after Woodson had a 20-yard head start. He also overtook Bobby Mitchell, certainly among the speediest players in professional football. Only he didn't grab Mitchell right away. Instead, he matched him stride for stride for a while, then bumped the runner out of bounds. When asked why he played it that way, Deacon dead-panned, "I just wanted to see who was faster. Now I know."

The "Deacon" nickname also came in for its share of kidding.

"Why is he praying?" was the standard question.

"So he won't kill anybody this afternoon," was the standard reply.

Small wonder Deacon Jones soon acquired a second nickname—Secretary of Defense.

In 1966, George Allen, a former assistant coach with the Chicago Bears, took command of the Rams, replacing Harland Svare. Perhaps the Rams were just fated to come alive by then.

Certainly Svare was as solid a coach as any in the league, and he had done much for the team. For whatever reason, Los Angeles left the cellar and began to climb. The Rams were third in the Western standings in 1966 with an 8–6–0 record. The defense was second to Green Bay in the entire NFL; the Rams yielded only 212 points in fourteen games, and that's just under 15 points per contest. The team looked like a winner again after the long drought.

Los Angeles was depending on a kind of "Front Five" when the 1967 training camp began. Roosevelt Grier had been in bad shape the previous year because of leg trouble, but it looked as if he might come back. But in an exhibition game against Kansas City, Grier suddenly fell to the ground. Nobody had touched him. His Achilles' tendon was torn. For Grier, the likable, music-loving, near-sighted giant, it was the end of a great career.

The Rams carried on with a vengeance, ripping off six consecutive preseason victories. Then they took on the brand-new New Orleans Saints, an expansion team with delusions of grandeur. The Saints had won five of six exhibition games, and for a while it seemed that this bunch of rejects might really get somewhere. The new boys took heart right off, when one of their rookies, John Gilliam, fielded the opening kickoff and raced ninety-four yards into the end zone!

However, the Saints put only six more points on the scoreboard, although they did almost score one more touchdown. Bill Kilmer, their quarterback, broke out of the pocket and ran thirty-one yards. But he fumbled away the football, and there were no more touchdown threats.

The front four and their sidekicks, meanwhile, were teaching the newcomers that they were still children and should mind their elders. On one series, the defense crashed in and dropped the Saints for three straight losses. Los Angeles won, 27–13.

Deacon Jones and his henchmen almost brutalized Minnesota in the second game of the season. In the first two quarters, the Vikings' running yardage stood at a big round zero! Jones and Olsen got to Joe Kapp for a safety, and then proceeded to knock him about some more, continuing their assault on two succeeding passers. In the third quarter Kapp connected with a bomb down to the Ram 18-yard line. Then Roger Brown steamrollered through to smear Kapp for a loss of 8, and the bruised Viking was promptly replaced. Los Angeles won, 39–3.

The Dallas Cowboys were also undefeated in regular season play when they tangled with the Rams. After it was over, the Cowboys were 2–1–0, the Rams 3–0–0. Even with Roger Brown lost for part of the game, Dallas couldn't run with the ball. It was one of the oddities of pro football. Don Perkins of the Cowboys totaled fifty-five yards in twelve carries; the rest of the Dallas ball carriers amassed *minus two yards!* Deacon Jones tossed the Cowboys' quarterback, Don Meredith, for eight yards, and Lundy reached his sub, Craig Morton, for eight more. But the Dallas Doomsday Defense equaled that. George Andrie and Bob Lilly smeared Roman Gabriel once each.

And then the defense fell apart. The Rams played the 49ers and blew a lead after having staged a magnificent come-from-behind effort. After trailing 20–0, they stormed back to take a 24–20 edge while the Fearsome Foursome held firm. The 49ers had possession, second-and-13. The Rams gambled with a safety blitz, and that was a mistake. San Francisco's quarterback John Brodie, threw into the vacated area, and there went the ball game. Furthermore, Brodie wasn't dumped even once.

Next came a lucky tie with the Colts. Johnny Unitas wasn't put down either. And the Colt star almost pulled the game out. On fourth-and-1, with the ball on the Los Angeles 14, he sent Ray Perkins under the crossbar and laid the ball right in his lap. Perkins dropped it. Tom Matte dropped the ball on the Ram 30. On the 5-yard line, Willie Richardson let a Johnny U pass roll off his fingertips. Finally, Unitas found Richardson, and Willie held on to the football—just long enough to be tackled and have the ball stolen from under his body by the Ram defensive back, Clarence Williams.

The Los Angeles front line continued to sputter, this time against Washington, and the result was another tie. Deacon Jones preserved the standoff, pushing the Redskins back fifteen yards in two plays during the final fifty seconds of the ballgame.

So, three games, one loss and two ties. Deacon Jones had the simple answer to the direct question, "What happened?" Snapped the Deak, "Man, we were just lousy, that's all!"

The Rams snapped out of it against the Chicago Bears. All they had to do was key in on Gale Sayers, and they did. The Chicago star was stopped cold, racking up thirteen yards in thirteen carries! In fact the big ground-gainer was Jack Concannon, the quarterback. Forced to leave the pocket by the Ram rush, Concannon slithered over the wet field for seventy-seven yards in eleven carries. In the end, the entire Bear rushing game netted exactly ninety-two yards.

Next came the 49ers again, and the Front Four continued to exert tremendous pressure on the passer. Those big guys were in on Brodie constantly, looming tall, leaping high to obscure his vision. Later, when asked about the Los Angeles line, Brodie remarked ruefully that they were so tall there seemed to be snow on their helmets. The Rams won, 17–7, against a stubborn San Francisco team that refused to fold no matter how hard it was hit.

The Philadelphia Eagles fell next, then the Atlantic Falcons, the Detroit Lions, and the Falcons again. During the six-game winning streak begun against the Bears, the Rams had yielded a grand total of fifty-four points—six touchdowns (plus conversions) and four field goals. Playing like inspired men, the Fearsome Foursome had blocked field goals, tossed the passer, stopped the running game, forced interceptions. Joe Kuharich, coach of the Philadelphia Eagles, put his finger on the Ram surge when he observed, "The Eagles couldn't put three good plays together. The Ram front four made all the difference."

All season the Rams had been confident of winning the NFL title. Their hopes had been jolted slightly by the loss and two ties. The Rams had spent their winning streak chasing the undefeated but tied Baltimore Colts, and as the end of the season neared, once more Los Angeles could smell first-place money. It was mathematically possible for the team to go all the way if it could win four more games, two in the regular season and two in the playoffs. A sweep could take the Rams into the Super Bowl.

The two regular season games were with Green Bay and Baltimore; then the Packers again, for they had won in the Central Division of the Western Conference. If the Rams got by the Pack, there was still the winner of the Dallas-Cleveland game, which decided the Eastern Conference title. What a brutal schedule!

Los Angeles played them one game at a time and got by the Packers, 27–24, pulling out the victory in the last thirty-five seconds. A blocked punt set up the victory. Bart Starr was dropped three times for a loss of eighteen yards and was forced to spend much of the time scrambling out of the pocket to avoid being blasted into the grandstand. The Packers' vaunted ground attack was blunted time and again. Jones-Olsen-Brown-Lundy were merely magnificent.

Immediately after the final whistle the Rams began to worry all over again. Especially the front four. Because no defensive line in its collective right mind enjoyed taking on the best passer in professional football, Johnny Unitas. He had completed one of his best years, guiding the Colts to an undefeated but twice-tied season. Johnny U had courage that bordered on the incredible. Even while the monsters of the line and the aggressive linebackers were boring in on him, he would stand there, holding the ball, waiting for a receiver to get that half step on a cornerback, waiting, waiting, until it seemed that he was about to be destroyed. And then he would fling the ball to his receivers as though it were a missile with radar laces. In a quiet, workmanlike, professional way, he made monkeys out of all front fours.

The Los Angeles game plan was simple enough. "Go harder! Harder!" George Allen kept telling that to his front four throughout the game. They had to reach Unitas. If he had time to throw he could pick apart any set of cornerbacks and safety men in the league.

The first time Baltimore had possession, Roger Brown charged through and dropped the passer. Baltimore finally had to punt, and the Rams got a field goal out of their march.

Unitas began to set up slightly deeper after that, and it took the line maybe half a second longer to reach him. For Johnny U that was like a two-week vacation, and he began to click off the passes. Baltimore hit for the touchdown and it was 7–3.

Gabriel got the touchdown back with a long one to Jack Snow. But Johnny Unitas chuckled at 10–7 leads. He had been known to engineer three touchdowns in a half-dozen minutes. He set about immediately to remedy the situation, and in a very short time the Colts were on the Ram 27, second-and-6. Unitas dropped back to pass; Jones and Olsen went smashing in with a tremendous burst of power. Deacon dove despairingly and managed to hit Unitas on the hips. Olsen got to him from the other side just as the ball was being released. The ball wobbled up and out high and hung there; Ed Meador of the Rams picked it off. Not only was the threat stopped but Los Angeles even went on to score.

If there was a turning point in the game, that was it. As Unitas had to take to the air more and more, the Ram front four grew bolder and bolder. Without the threat of the run to bother them much, they could concentrate on the pass rush. And Unitas was trying to throw deep. He had to wait the half-second for his receivers to get farther downfield. The half-second gave the Rams a shade more time to reach him. And they did.

In the previous eighteen games of the season (including exhibitions), Unitas had been put down only thirteen times. In the final game of the season, he was spilled seven times! The game turned into a 34–10 rout as the game but helpless Johnny U was hurried and rushed and tossed all over the field.

After the game, which eliminated Baltimore from the playoffs, the battered Unitas said, "They were murder. They're in on you all the time, and when they hit you, you feel it. I'll try not to think of those four so-and-sos all summer, but I guess I will." The happy Ram coach, George Allen, said, "I think that was one of the finest games the front four has played."

So it was on to that refrigerator sometimes known as the State of Wisconsin for the Western Conference title game against Green Bay. The temperature at Milwaukee County Stadium stood at 20 degrees, but the 12-mile-an-hour wind sweeping across the turf made it much colder.

The Ram four was up against what was probably the best offensive line in pro football. From tackle to tackle, the line of Bob Skoronski, Gale Gillingham, Ken Bowman, Jerry Kramer, and Forrest Gregg had height, weight, strength, and experience. They could pass block and go forward on the straight-ahead rush with equal facility.

The game started off as advertised. Neither team penetrated deep into the other's territory. Once Roger Brown broke in and sacked Bart Starr for a loss of 11. The Green Bay front four didn't let Roman Gabriel take his time either. Obviously this game was going to be decided by hard line play, a break-the-game-open run or pass, a couple of fortunate fumbles. That's what happened.

Late in the first period Starr hit Carroll Dale with a 9-yard pass. Dale fumbled when hit, Los Angeles recovered. Then a short pass and a face-mask penalty gained 20 yards, a line buck took 3 more, and Gabriel's pass to Bernie Casey went for the touchdown with 44 seconds left in the quarter.

Two sparkling runs got the touchdown back in the second quarter. First, Tommy Brown fielded a punt on his own 15 and raced all the way to the Los Angeles 46 before he was brought down. Then Travis Williams, the Green Bay speedster, took a handoff and sliced around right tackle. Jerry Kramer, the all-pro guard, blocked out Merlin Olsen while Deacon Jones was double-teamed by Gillingham and Gregg. Williams never stopped running until he had crossed the Rams' goal.

Although that run only tied the score, it seemed to shake up the Los Angeles defense, both up front and in the secondary. It was as though they were trying to figure out what had gone wrong. And while they were wondering, Green Bay scored again the next time it got the football. In nine plays the Packers dented the Los Angeles end zone for the second time.

After that it was all Packers. They had the momentum, and it was their line hitting Gabriel as the Fearsome Foursome let the ballgame slip away. In the third period, the Rams had the ball for three series of plays. In each of those sequences, the Packer forward wall wrapped up the passer. Henry Jordan got through, and it resulted in a loss of 8 yards. Willie Davis cracked in, and it was minus 9. Jordan grabbed Gabriel for 12 more. Starr, on the other hand, let his runners run and his receivers receive. The Rams finished out the game as though in a dream. When the gun mercifully sounded, the Pack was leading 28–7, and a Gabriel pass had just been intercepted.

Let the record show that the Los Angeles Rams picked themselves up from defeat and went on to give a strong account of themselves in the next two years. In 1968 they were second in defense in the Western Conference, but only because Baltimore tied the defensive record that year. In 1969 they were fourth. The line was older, perhaps a step slower. But nobody ever took too many liberties with that great Los Angeles line. Because, year in and year out, the Fearsome Foursome was right up there among the leaders, a growling, ferocious force to be reckoned with in that front-line area known as the pit.

Braase, Miller, and Two Guys Named Smith

GREAT DEFENSIVE LINEMEN ARE NOTHING new for the Baltimore Colts. Over the years they have boasted some of the very best in football. They have arrived singly, in pairs, or in bunches, and all the top ones will be talked about until the day people stop discussing football. As an example, think about two of the all-time all-pros, Gino Marchetti and Gene "Big Daddy" Lipscomb.

It would not be totally incorrect to say that Gino Marchetti was a "3-H" lineman. He played with his head, his hands—and his heart. Marchetti wasn't overpoweringly strong, nor very fast, and at 240 pounds he didn't intimidate anyone through sheer bulk. But his fantastic *desire* made him invincible. Many times he would be blocked out of a play, but he would get up, pursue, and bring down the ball carrier with an incredible second effort. He didn't hand-fight, he clawed. He didn't blitz, he hurricaned. He didn't tackle, he surrounded. When his leg was broken in one game, he refused to be carried into the dressing room. Instead he lay on a stretcher along the sidelines, screaming to his teammates to win, to win, to win. There are many who say that Marchetti was the best defensive end in the history of football. There are few who wouldn't get into an argument trying to refute that claim. Twice Marchetti tried to retire, and both times he listened to the siren song of the Colt front office, saying the team couldn't get along without him— and it could not. When he did call it quits, he left a hole in the line that was almost impossible to fill.

Big Daddy Lipscomb wasn't cut from the same bolt as Marchetti but he was just as great. In Lipscomb's case it was a matter of brute strength overpowering all comers. As a rule, when running backs or offensive linemen feel they are unfairly abused or hit with unnecessary force, they will square off against their opponents and offer to fight. But never against Big Daddy. If—inadvertently, to be sure—he mistreated anyone during a play, the unhappy victim nursed his bruises and walked away, mindful of the fact that the bruises could become permanent injuries if Big Daddy were aroused. Even the fantastic Jimmy Brown, undoubtedly the greatest running back football has produced, a man who feared nothing that moved, breathed, or wore man-made clothing, was careful how he spoke to Big Daddy. When Lipscomb tackled him, Brown would slowly arise and say, "Nice play, Gene. You're really on your toes today."

"Really, Jim?" Big Daddy would reply in all his childlike, delighted innocence. "I'm goin' good today, huh?"

"Like always," Brown would say. "Keep workin'."

Perhaps Brown was psyching Lipscomb. Or else he was being prudent. If Lipscomb was calm and kindly disposed toward Brown, the running back knew the full fury of the man would not descend on him the next time they collided, and that was a prime requisite for survival when playing against Lipscomb. He was probably the strongest man in the league in his playing days.

The Colts won a number of titles with Marchetti and Lipscomb in the pit. It would be ridiculous to imply that the defense did it all, especially in view of the fact that the incomparable Johnny Unitas was at quarterback, passing his opponents dizzy. But that defensive line sure was a comfort to the Baltimore coach and a pain to the opposing offense.

The 1968 Colt front four did not include any superstars of the Marchetti-Lipscomb caliber. How often do such players come along anyway? But, when talking about the best defensive lines in football, that one must be included, and ranked high on the list.

At one end of the line was Ordell Braase, 6 feet 4 inches tall and 242 pounds. His success is particularly heartwarming because it proves that nice guys *can* finish first. Braase didn't figure in Baltimore's plans at first. He was a fourteenth draft choice, and had been a pretty good lineman at the University of South Dakota but certainly no national headline-grabber. Braase had to report to ROTC camp before checking in at the 1954 summer training camp and lost some practice time. He wouldn't have stayed anyway, because the coaches told him he was too light to play in a pro line. Braase went into the Army, came out in 1957 and tried again. By then he had increased his weight to 225 pounds, and the Colts kept him around as a substitute defensive end. Through constant improvement—and some added weight—he took over as a regular in 1960.

Braase played at the other end of the line from Gino Marchetti, and naturally he was lost in the shadow of the superstar's work. At least, he seldom received the plaudits handed out to Marchetti. But the Colts knew how good he was, and the first one to praise Braase was Marchetti. Said Gino of Ordell, "Well, if I am the best defensive end in pro football, then I guess Braase must be the second best." A lot of other football people thought so too.

According to one hard-bitten school of football philosophy,

it's perfectly all right for a player to break the rules—or bend them a little—provided he doesn't get caught. Braase thought otherwise. A devout Christian, he played as hard as anyone on the field, but if he did anything illegal it was strictly an accident. Violence for its own sake was beyond his understanding.

In 1961, a Los Angeles Rams lineman, Roy Hord, let go with a hard forearm shot to the face that broke Braase's jaw. Another player might have nursed a grudge and devised ways to retaliate. Not Ordell Braase. The next time they lined up against each other, Braase played his normal tough game. Hord walked off the field after the game with only the usual number of bruises.

On another occasion, playing against the Lions, Braase had his man beaten, only to feel a hand gripping his jersey. Braase didn't chew him out. He said to his opponent, "I'm surprised that a man with your ability has to stoop to a cheap trick like that to stop me." Ashamed, the player did no more holding that day.

Playing tackle for the Colts was Billy Ray Smith, an all-around athlete from the University of Arkansas. A third draft choice of the Rams in 1956, Billy Ray later went to the Pittsburgh Steelers and then to Baltimore. He was a defensive end, but when Big Daddy Lipscomb was traded to Pittsburgh, Billy Ray took his spot. At 6 feet 4 inches, he was tall enough, but at 235 pounds a trifle on the light side. His good moves and excellent hand agility more than made up for lack of heft. Smith, in fact, used his hands better than many other defensive linemen, for he had been a college champion and Golden Gloves boxer. Perhaps he might have even considered a boxing career, except that Pete Rademacher, who later fought for the heavyweight title, got Billy Ray into the ring and threw a few punches at him. Billy Ray changed his mind.

Somewhere along the way Smith picked up the nickname "The Rabbit." According to one version of the story, it was because he looked like Bugs Bunny. He was also called "Br'er

Rabbit" in college, probably because of his initials. He liked to clown, needle people, make them laugh. But there was nothing timid or funny about the way he tackled people on a football field.

The tackle spot opened up temporarily when Billy Ray retired after the 1962 season. He said that business interests required his full time, but perhaps his decision was hastened by a painful back injury sustained against the 49ers. He didn't play in 1963.

That was when Fred Miller came to the Colts. A 6-foot 3-inch 245-pounder, he had been captain of the "Chinese Bandits," the name hung on the Louisiana State University defensive team, although Miller himself was a two-way lineman. Quiet, easy-going, Miller had been good enough to be named to the college all-star team and played a whale of a game. He wasn't spectacular, but he got results.

At first Billy Ray's job fell to Miller, and he proved himself worthy of a regular assignment even when Smith came out of retirement the following year, because he just couldn't stay away from football.

Miller, Marchetti, Braase, and Smith, plus Lou Michaels, John Diehl, and Guy Reese became the Baltimore front four, and played outstanding football. But when Marchetti quit for good in 1966, there was a gaping hole at end. Coach Don Shula had several options for filling it, including Andy Stynchula (obtained from the Giants), Lou Michaels, and Roy Hilton. And, as insurance for the aging Billy Ray, he drafted the best college lineman in the country, a 6-foot 7-inch, 290-pound monster named Charles "Bubba" Smith.

Merely to look at Bubba was to be intimidated. Other college teams simply quit running plays over his side of the line. In a game against Ohio State, he personally ruined the enemy ground game; Ohio ended up with a *minus twenty-two yards* rushing! And he was stunningly fast. During a break in Michigan State practice, Bubba challenged the backfield to a series of races. He beat the quarterback, Steve Juday, by five yards and the fullback, Eddie Cotton, by four yards in a fifty-yard dash. That was no disgrace because Bubba was faster than most of the country's college running backs. Playing against Penn State, he chased and caught Mike Irwin from behind after Irwin had outrun everyone else. The combination of speed and brute power made him unstoppable. Michigan State students took to chanting, "Kill, Bubba! Kill!"

In the 1967 all-star game, Bubba was matched against Jerry Kramer, Green Bay's all-time, all-pro offensive lineman. Afterward, Kramer said that when Bubba learned to overcome his eagerness, he would undoubtedly be one of the best defensive linemen in pro football.

Pro veterans like nothing better than to deflate the big college stars, and the Colts began to needle Bubba when he arrived at the training camp. Billy Ray, the "other Smith," didn't seem in the least worried that Bubba might take his job away. Said Billy Ray, "He'll be good some day, but right now I've got experience, and that's like gold in this league."

Billy Ray was right. In a preseason game, Bubba wrenched his knee, and he wasn't in playing shape for a long time. Besides, tackle was not his normal position; he was an end and couldn't get the feel of the new position. And so the college phenomenon Bubba Smith became a bench spectator.

When Bubba did crack the lineup, he showed flashes of his old power and speed. He got into the Atlanta game and sacked the quarterback three times. But he never did move Billy Ray off the regular line. Experience *was* as good as gold.

Brooding Bubba got some good news before the 1968 season began. Don Shula called and told him that the defensive end position was open if he could win it. The Colts' coach realized that Bubba had too much potential to waste his time picking up bench splinters, and maybe the brass had made a mistake trying to switch him to tackle. For Bubba it was a breeze. And Baltimore got off winging.

Records can be deceiving. The Colts had a five-game winning streak before the rest of the league took a deep breath, but the club looked ragged even with its perfect record. Only against Pittsburgh did it look sharp, but that was no yardstick because everybody else was beating the Steelers. To listen to the Colts, no one would suspect they were walking on eggshells; but they were.

It has been truly said that no team is better than its quarterback, and in Johnny Unitas the Colts had the best in football. It would be a waste of time to cite any of his records; anyone who knows what a football looks like also knows about Johnny U. When he hurt his arm in an exhibition game, every resident of Baltimore turned sickly green. How could anybody replace the best in the business?

Fortunately, Baltimore had picked up Earl Morrall shortly before. Morrall, a journeyman passer who had been traded around the league every couple of years, had just been dropped by the New York Giants and was ready to call it a career. Shula persuaded him to hang on at least one more year. Substituting for Unitas was a dead-end job, but Morrall listened to Shula's blandishments.

An in-and-outer before, Morrall suddenly caught fire. Maybe it was the protection he got. With Unitas gone, the Colt offensive line guarded him as if his throwing arm were the crown jewels. Or maybe, after all the bitter disappointments of his pro career, Morrall was overdue for a fine year. True, he was no Unitas, but then again, nobody else was either.

The sixth and seventh games on the schedule were against Cleveland and Los Angeles. Seasoned professionals play the games one at a time, because a football can take peculiar bounces. The Colts seemed to forget about that. They psyched themselves up for the Ram game, because the Rams had knocked them out of contention in the showdown game of the previous year. So, while the Colts were thinking about the Rams, Cleveland administered a sound thrashing, 30–20. Gone was the unbeaten season. Baltimore's front four looked ragged, lethargic—the whole team did. Braase and the others got to the Cleveland passer twice for eleven yards, but when it counted, the Browns' quarterback seemed to have as much time as he needed.

This time it was the Rams who came to town undefeated, leading the Colts by a game. A loss would drop the Colts two back, almost out of the race. The Rams, charging ahead with a fourteen-game regular-season winning streak (eight from the previous year), would have the momentum, while two defeats in a row would undoubtedly leave Baltimore dispirited, sagging, with morale low.

The full responsibility for victory fell on the shoulders of the defensive linemen. They had to hold the score down, because the Ram lines, offensive and defensive, were considered the best in the NFL. In six games, the Los Angeles quarterback had been dropped only four times. And in those six games, enemy runners had gained an average of 62.5 yards per game running against the Fearsome Foursome. Small wonder then that the Rams were unbeaten. Nobody could run against them, and nobody could reach the passer.

Baltimore took care of those statistics in great style. In the first half alone, Roman Gabriel was creamed four times, with Fred Miller and a linebacker, Mike Curtis, leading the charge. In those two periods Gabriel's passing picked up 29 yards. But he had also been thrown for losses totaling 29 yards. Therefore, at half time, the Ram aerial gains stood at exactly zero!

Grabbing the passer was only part of the rush put on by the Colt four. They rushed Gabriel and the running backs unmercifully, forcing hurried passes, driving back the runners. The Colts scored one touchdown when Curtis tackled the ball carrier, causing a fumble. Miller caught the ball and raced to the Ram 4. Morrall himself carried it over.

To give him credit, Roman Gabriel showed great courage

and strength. Time and again the 220-pound quarterback broke tackles as he ran and dodged and scrambled, trying to get the pass off. This was the Baltimore defensive line at its best.

The offense wasn't bad either. Supposedly, the Rams were a team that no backfield set could run against. Baltimore did and, what's more, totaled 159 yards, almost three times what other clubs had managed to pick up on the ground. The final score was 27–10, Colts, and they had put on a very impressive show indeed.

In the second half of the season, the Baltimore defense was easily the best in professional football. It began showing its true class against the Giants with a 26–0 shutout.

It was the first whitewash job on the Giants in five years, but even the four zeros on the scoreboard didn't tell what really happened. The scrambling Fran Tarkenton was flattened twice and intercepted once. He completed ten for twenty, but his total gain in the air was ninety-eight yards, meaning that he couldn't take the time to set up for the bomb and had to dunk off the short ones to his safety valves. The Baltimore four put on quite a show.

Next came a 27–10 win over the Lions. Four times they got to the passer. When Detroit got tough and started to march, the Colt front four got tougher, especially deep in their own territory.

Another shutout followed, 27–0 over St. Louis, the second in three games by the Colt defenses. And it was the first time the Cardinals had been held scoreless in six years. Braase, Miller, Smith, and Smith put such a rush on Jim Hart that the Cards never got closer than Baltimore's 29-yard line. The safety blitz was devastating, and the front four were in the Cardinal backfield so much it seemed as if they were wearing St. Louis uniforms. Hart went seventeen for forty-seven attempts. St. Louis gained just fifty-eight yards trying to dent the forward wall on the ground. On average, the Cards advanced the ball exactly 2.9 yards with each snap from center.

The Minnesota Vikings were next, and this was another of those clashes between great front fours. But the Colts rose to the occasion and smeared the Viking passer five times for a total loss of thirty-nine yards. Their rush was stupendous—that's the only word for it.

Not that the Minnesota charge was lacking. Carl Eller tore in and belted Earl Morrall loose from the football on the Baltimore 24. Soon the Vikings had a first-and-10 on the Colts' 10-yard line. But the Colts put on a goal-line stand that warmed the hearts of all spectators, no matter which team they rooted for.

A line buck gained 2 yards; a pass put the ball on the 1. In such situations, a team with good running backs calls on the power play. Minnesota's Bill Brown was a past master of the line plunge. The thick-legged fullback had already scored twelve touchdowns, eleven of them rushing. From close in he was especially deadly.

Brown took the handoff and tore forward. Fred Miller broke in, pursued and caught Brown from the side, dropping him for no gain. Once more Brown got the ball and rammed straight ahead. The entire forward wall—front four and linebackers alike—rose up to greet him. Brown was stopped on the ½-yard line! Baltimore took over.

And those two stops were money plays. Baltimore was leading, 21–9 (which turned out to be the final score). Had Brown cracked in and the conversion been added, the score would have been 21–16 with 12 minutes left to play. Baltimore played a ball-control game, and the next time the Vikings got the ball, there were only 4 minutes left on the clock. Those twelve points were just too much to overcome. Minnesota had to play long-bomb football to score again, but Baltimore was ready and shut the door.

Atlanta was next, and when the smoke of battle had cleared, Baltimore had another shutout. The score was 44–0! The Colts' domination of the Falcons was complete, overwhelming. Big Bubba had long established himself as one of the most feared ends in the business, and he recovered a fumble that day. The Colt line dropped Randy Johnson and Bob Berry four times for a loss of forty-nine yards, and when they weren't knocking down the passers they were harassing them to the point of neurosis. The Baltimore defenses engulfed the passers and runners in a tidal wave of Colt jerseys. It seemd as if there were two or three men in on every tackle.

Then Green Bay put its collective head on the chopping block. The two-time former Super Bowl champions were outclassed all the way as the Colt front four creamed Bart Starr. The vaunted running attack and ball-control game went nowhere as the Pack was limited to sixty-six yards rushing. Green Bay managed to hit for a field goal, but that was all. It was 16–3, Colts.

Meanwhile, Los Angeles was being upset by Chicago, and that put the Rams out of the running.

For the second time that year Baltimore had put together six consecutive victories, and it had been one of the most remarkable winning streaks on record, a tribute to an airtight defense. In those six games the opposition had scored exactly twenty-two points! Only once had the Colt goal line been crossed; five times the enemy had been forced to settle for a field goal. Forgotten—at least temporarily—were the fine front fours of the Rams, Vikings, Packers, and Chiefs. This one—Braase, Miller, and two guys named Smith—was the best of all. Just look at the statistics!

The regular season wrap-up against Los Angeles wasn't quite meaningless, even though it didn't mean much in the standings. But Baltimore did have a chance to beat the record of Chicago's 1963 defensive unit, which had allowed 144 points over the season. All the Colts needed was a reasonable effort. But they couldn't make it. The aroused Rams dented Baltimore for twenty-four points, and although the Colts won the game, they, too, ended up with 144 points scored against them; all they could do was tie the record.

But the final tally showed them with a 13–1–0 won-lost total. It tied the best fourteen-game record in the NFL, set by Green Bay in 1962.

The football season wasn't quite over. There were playoffs on tap: first, for the Western Conference championship against Minnesota, and then with the Eastern Conference winner (it turned out to be Cleveland), and finally, the Super Bowl for the whole ball of wax.

The Colt-Viking game was a dandy, and the 60,238 fans who sat through it in a cold driving rain with winds gusting to 14 miles an hour got their money's worth. It was billed as a battle of defensive lines, and the drumbeaters weren't exaggerating.

The first period was scoreless as the clubs didn't threaten too much. Baltimore began moving in the second quarter, and it took three passes to score. Two of them went to Willie Richardson, who made spectacular catches of both. A short one to Tom Mitchell accounted for the touchdown, the only one in the half.

In the third quarter the Vikings tried a blitz on Earl Morrall, and it cost them. Seven men went piling in on him. He rolled out and spotted John Mackey loose over the middle. Morrall lofted a floater over the outstretched hands of Minnesota's Roy Winston. Mackey broke two tackles and went all the way.

Joe Kapp tried to lead the Vikings back, but this time the Colts pulled the blitz on him. No fewer than nine men broke through. Billy Ray hit Kapp's legs, Bubba slammed into his chest; the ball popped loose and the linebacker Mike Curtis fielded it like a fly ball. He was ten yards ahead of his pursuers when he started toward pay dirt and he was still ten yards ahead over the finish line.

And that was the ballgame. Joe Kapp tried a lot of desperation passes and did manage to connect a couple of times. But in the final moments of the last series, the Viking quarterback was thrown twice.

Still, if Kapp was treated roughly, you should have seen the other guy. Minnesota's Purple People Eaters spilled the Baltimore quarterback four times. They didn't disgrace themselves by any means, in spite of the 24–14 score.

Finally, the Colts took on Cleveland for the NFL title. The Browns were the only club to have beaten Baltimore, and Shula's boys wanted revenge badly. They got it, too.

A combination of forces pitched in to trounce Cleveland. It was partly the Browns' own fault and partly the effort of the Baltimore defensive unit, and Blanton Collier's forces never had a chance. Just to give a couple of examples of how events ganged up on Cleveland:

In the first half, Bubba Smith brushed aside a few Browns and got inside to block Don Cockroft's field-goal attempt.

In the second half, on one series Leroy Kelly was stopped for no gain by Fred Miller. Then Miller and Ordell Braase got in to flatten the quarterback, Bill Nelsen, for a 13-yard loss. So Cleveland punted, and ten plays later, after a 64-yard drive, Baltimore had the touchdown.

Also in the second half, a Nelsen-to-Warfield pass that produced a big gain was called back because a Cleveland player was caught holding, and that was their own fault. The Browns picked up 5 on a line play, but that was instantly nullified when Braase put down Nelsen for a 7-yard loss. With a fourth-and-29 situation, what else could Cleveland do but punt? So, seven plays and 48 yards later, the Colts had another touchdown.

Cleveland got the ball. The backup quarterback, Bill Ryan, fumbled the snap from center, and Baltimore's linebacker, Don Shinnick, recovered. It was just that kind of a day. And when it was over, the Colts had one more shutout, 34–0!

And finally there was a team other than Green Bay representing the National Football League in the Super Bowl. The Baltimore Colts were there partly because Earl Morrall, a retread quarterback, had come through with a remarkable effort, which won for him the Most Valuable Player award, and partly because of a determined offensive brigade, but mostly because of an outstanding defensive platoon, highlighted by the best front four in football—at least for 1968. And in the hearts and minds of every Baltimore Colt was the deep certainty that they were vastly superior to their opponents from the American Football League, the New York Jets.

Maybe they were. In one game, any number of accidents can happen, any number of slips and mistakes and bad breaks. It's no big secret that the Jets beat Baltimore, 16–7. But *how* New York won—that's something else.

It is said that Joe Namath made the supreme sacrifice for this Super Bowl game. He forsook the flock of miniskirted cuties who usually hung around his neck like a string of peace beads, and with his coach, Weeb Ewbank, studied the films of Baltimore games. He saw that the Baltimore secondary made peculiar moves when throwing the safety blitz. The safety would creep up slowly until he could almost pat his linebackers on the butt. If there was no audible called by the quarterback, he went in. If there was an audible, he retreated, thinking that he had been spotted and the play was coming his way.

So Namath used a lot of dummy huddles, calling no play at all. The play itself was called at the line of scrimmage, but it didn't sound like an audible changing the play that had been called in the huddle.

Also, the Jet brass came to the conclusion that maybe Ordell Braase, the right end, and Don Shinnick, the right linebacker, were getting old and tired, and maybe the strain of six preseason games, fourteen regular season games and two playoff games—a total of twenty-two bruising games of football—might have taken some of the starch out of them. Both were twelve-year veterans; Braase was thirty-six years old, Shinnick thirty-three, and that's getting right up there in athletics. It might be possible to run against that side of the line with some degree of success. It was a surprising gamble in view of the great job both men had done all season long, but the Jets were given practically no chance to win anyway, and that seemed to be as good a game plan as any.

It took some time for the Jets to act on their ideas, and at first they went nowhere. While the line was shutting off the running game, the Colts lost a golden opportunity to score when Lou Michaels missed an easy field goal from the 27-yard line.

In the second period, Namath and his crew began to make it all happen, and they picked on the right side of the Colt line. Matt Snell did it all—finding out that maybe Baltimore *was* relatively weaker—in that direction. He pounded the line four times for gains of 1, 7, 6, and 12 yards.

Then Namath began to throw in both directions, and Snell ran left and right, and finally, from 4 yards out, Snell ran and skidded and whirled in for the touchdown.

Applying the pressure in the third quarter, Joe Willie Namath kept probing the line, particularly in the direction of Braase and Shinnick. He wasn't always successful; once big Bubba Smith crashed in and flattened him for a loss of 9. But twice he got into field-goal range and both times Jim Turner cashed in.

By the fourth quarter it was 16-0 as Turner hit again from 9 yards out. Morrall had long since been replaced by the willing but still sore-armed Unitas, and near the end Johnny U led his team to a touchdown. But the game was history by then, both clubs merely going through the motions.

Did the right side of the Colt line fold up, lose its grip, and let the game slip away? Well, yes and no. A team scoring sixteen points in a game isn't overpowering *anybody* with its offense. Much of the time Braase and Shinnick were in there to stop the runner or receiver. But sometimes—often enough—Snell did run on them, and he did gain yardage, and he did score the Jets' sole touchdown through that alley.

And yet Baltimore could have won the game. Twice the Colts had touchdowns set up, and some little thing prevented them. Early in the second period, Morrall sent Tom Mitchell into the end zone. For just a split second he was clear of Randy Beverly, and Morrall threw. But football is a game of split seconds, and either Morrall threw too soon or Mitchell turned too late. The ball hit the receiver's shoulder, bounced up and was picked off by Beverly.

The final play of the half was one of those screwball "flea-flicker" plays that every club has in its offensive arsenal, but is seldom used because it involves tossing the ball back and forth like a basketball. Morrall took the snap, handed off to Tom Matte, who passed the ball back to Morrall, who flipped out to Jerry Hill, the running back. But it didn't work because Hill was in a crowd of Jets, and Jim Hudson intercepted. Meanwhile, there was Jimmy Orr all alone in the end zone, waving his arms frantically, and not a single Jet within 20 yards of him. Morrall just didn't see him.

Some second-guessers nod their heads wisely and say that the Jets didn't win the game, that Baltimore lost it. To some extent that's true. The Colts missed good opportunities. But then, all teams do that in a game. That's football.

Other Monday-morning quarterbacks are convinced that Joe Namath psyched the Colts. He passed magnificently for the Jets, and he could read the Colt defenses as if they were a newspaper headline. That's true too. Who would argue that Joe Willie doesn't rate with the best field generals in the pros?

They'll be talking about that game for a long time.

The Purple People Eaters

IN 1964, THE MINNESOTA VIKINGS DEFEATED the San Francisco 49ers, 27–22, no thanks to the Vikings' defensive lineman Jim Marshall. The 49ers' quarterback, George Mira, had just flipped a pass to Bill Kilmer out in the flat. Kilmer was tackled, he fumbled, and Marshall picked up the loose football. Like a locomotive going down a steep grade, he rumbled sixty-six yards into the end zone. But, as he was negotiating the distance, he saw his teammate Fran Tarkenton shouting at him from the bench; he couldn't hear the Minnesota quarterback because the crowd was screaming too. When Marshall crossed the goal line, he was joyfully hugged by Bruce Bosley, one of the San Francisco players. At that instant, Marshall realized why Tarkenton was screaming and why Bosley was so happy.

He had run the wrong way! He had scored for the other side!

•

Alan Page, all-American defensive lineman, realized one of his ambitions when he was chosen to play in the 1967 All-Star game against the champion Green Bay Packers. Page knew that the Packer offensive line was strong, rugged, tricky. He also had the idea that he knew how to play football. When it was over, he found out how much he still had to learn.

"They didn't overpower me," he said morosely. "I wasn't even hit very hard. They just kept getting in my way and I couldn't go anywhere. They handled me like I was nothing."

•

When Gary Larsen played for the Los Angeles Rams, he was permitted to start just one game, against Green Bay. His opponent on the other side of the line was Forrest Gregg, whose name appeared on the all-pro list year after year. Gregg made him look like the inexperienced sub he was, bottling him up, working him over, keeping Larsen far, far away from the quarterback. It was a bad day for Larsen.

•

In Carl Eller's rookie year with the Vikings, he learned that football rules are not always enforced. Sometimes the officials don't see everything that's happening. Playing against the Chicago Bears, he beat the opposing tackle on one play, and was headed into the Chicago backfield when his opponent reached out and grabbed his legs.

"Hey," roared Eller, "you can't do that!"

"Yeah," said the tackle, "but I just did, man."

•

On opening day of the 1969 season, the heavily favored Vikings took on the New York Giants. Minnesota wanted to win this one badly for several reasons: first, of course, every team wants to win every football game; second, it would be a nice way to start the year, with a satisfying win; and third, playing against them was their former teammate, Fran Tarkenton.

For fifty-seven and one-half minutes the Vikings looked like winners. Five times the Giant quarterback had to throw under pressure, one pass was deflected by Alan Page, and twice the Viking foursome dumped Tarkenton.

But Tarkenton had also been causing them trouble all afternoon. Not that he had been so spectacularly successful; he'd done all right, and the Giants had two touchdowns and a field goal, even though they were losing, 23–17. But those Vikings were tired of chasing him. Tarkenton was one of the best scramblers in the business—indeed, there were defensive linemen who swore that he had invented the run-for-your-life brand of quarterbacking.

Once more, in the waning moments, the Giants mounted an attack. Tarkenton dropped back, saw his blocking disintegrate, and began zig-zagging all over the chalk marks, hotly pursued by four burly Viking tacklers. Just before he was swarmed under, Tarkenton let fly a high, arching pass in the general direction of the Minnesota goal. Two Vikings and two Giants leaped high. The ball popped up and fell into the hands of a Giant tight end, Butch Wilson, who stepped across into the end zone. Final score, 24–23, in favor of the Giants—a tremendous upset.

It had been a hard-luck loss for Minnesota. Somehow, the team always seemed touched by misfortune at the wrong time, what with injuries to key men, the loss of close games, a bad bounce of the football. And the learning process had taken time; mistakes had cost the club any number of crucial games.

But after the loss to the Giants that September day, everything seemed to change for the better. Throughout the rest of the regular season the Minnesota Vikings became one of the best and luckiest teams in professional football. It was as if a benevolent fate had decreed that the football should start taking bounces their way; and natural talent did the rest. When the Vikings didn't get the breaks naturally, they forced them. Most of the forcing was done by their great defensive line. And already this group of muscled men had acquired all sorts of nicknames, such as "Viking Vultures," "Four Norsemen," and "Purple People Eaters."

In one way this line was different from other great forward walls. The Vikings really had a "front five." Besides the usual regulars—Carl Eller, Alan Page, Jim Marshall, and Gary Larsen—there was one other man who got into most of the games when one of the tackles needed a breather. He was Paul Dickson, the "swingman." Once Dickson, too, had been a regular, playing alongside Jim Marshall. In fact Dickson and Marshall were there when the Minnesota Vikings were born in 1961.

It has been said that every man can write a book about the things that have happened to him in a lifetime. In that case a dozen books could have been written about Jim Marshall before he reached the age of thirty.

First, it was amazing that he was alive and well and able to chase Tarkenton, or other quarterbacks, or running backs. It was astonishing that someone who had been almost given up for dead should have the strength and quickness and balance to play head-to-head against the 260-pounders of the offensive lines. That he had survived at all was a tribute to his fighting spirit and refusal to quit against almost insurmountable odds.

As a kid in Columbus, Ohio, he got into gang fights, stole hubcaps, was a bookmaker. In a street fight he threw rocks and bricks—"alley apples" he called such missiles. But he was also tough enough to knock heads with anyone, anywhere. Once a bunch of kids challenged him, and Marshall ran from the fight. His father, a truck driver who knew what it was to scrape and scramble for a living, ordered the boy to go back and face them. He did, and whipped them all, taking on the whole group alone.

Sometimes he escaped with his life only by a fluke. Once he was in an automobile accident in which one man was killed. Somehow, Marshall managed to walk out of the collision unhurt. Another time he was playfully flipping grapes into the air and catching them in his mouth. One grape slid down his windpipe. Gasping and choking, Marshall was rushed to a hospital, where the grape was removed. On another occasion he was sitting in his car, fooling around with a loaded gun. He thought it was jammed and tried to extract the bullets. The gun went off and one of the slugs lodged in his abdomen. Yet all these accidents were almost minor, compared with the frightening illness that almost killed him.

Before Marshall's brushes with death, he had been one of the finest young junior athletes in the United States. He made the football team at Columbus East High School, where the line averaged 220 pounds per man—it was bigger and heavier than the line at Ohio State! Also on that team was Bernie Casey, who went on to the San Francisco 49ers and was rated as one of the best wide receivers in the NFL.

Marshall won his letters in football and track and field. He was all-state tackle when he graduated. Also, he was state champion in the discus throw and runner-up in shot-put. He was a high-jumper, and he ran the 100, the 220, and 440. Some forty colleges came to his door waving scholarships. Marshall wanted to go to Dartmouth, but he had loafed too much in class and his grades weren't good enough. He ended up at Ohio State.

As a sophomore, Marshall was one of the big reasons for State's trip to the Rose Bowl. In his junior year he showed promise of even bigger things. Against Purdue he scored two touchdowns, one on an interception, the other on a fumble recovery.

Marshall never did become a senior. There was money to be made in Canadian football, and when the Saskatchewan Rough Riders offered him $9,000, plus a bonus of $1,000, he grabbed it. Marshall played offensive and defensive tackle and offensive end. He did all right, too, catching three touchdown passes during the season.

The Cleveland Browns signed him, and he was a sub behind Paul Wiggin. Then he went into the Army. One month before his discharge he began to have headaches, which he thought were caused by his sinuses. Marshall didn't want to hang around in the Army, so he said nothing to the medics about those maddening pains. And that almost cost him his life. In the Browns' training camp he fell apart completely. Specialists diagnosed his illness as encephalitis, a brain disease that can kill or paralyze the victim.

For weeks he was in a semicoma. In his bookie days, Marshall wouldn't have risked a bet on his chances. But he pulled out of it on sheer grit.

When he returned to the Browns as offensive tackle, Marshall was still so weak that the defensive boys flicked him aside with a twitch of the hand. Cleveland saw an opportunity to unload him on the Vikings, and in 1961 Marshall found himself in Minnesota.

Yet, despite all the adversity, Jim Marshall could laugh at the bad breaks. After his wrong-way run in the San Francisco game, Marshall was invited to a luncheon by the Bonehead Club in Dallas, Texas. On the way to the airport, his cab was trapped in a traffic jam. He reached the plane barely in time, but the jet was rerouted to Chicago and set down with a faulty engine. Marshall arrived in Dallas at four o'clock. Naturally, the papers played it up as another wrong-way run.

Then he went into business selling wigs. Almost immediately the ladies began to scream about wrong shades and other boners. Marshall promptly gave up, keeping as much dignity as possible. "Women," he said gravely, "are too dangerous!"

Paul Dickson was another charter member of both the Vikings and the Hard Luck Club. A former mathematics major at Baylor University, he had received all-America mention and was the No. 1 draft choice of the Los Angeles Rams. Dickson came up as an offensive tackle; in fact, before he came to the Vikings, he had never played a minute of football on defense.

With the Rams in 1959, Dickson just couldn't put it all together. Shoving people around in the Southwest Conference was far easier than blocking the big guys in the pros. Somehow, all of a sudden, he just wasn't comfortable, and he didn't know why.

The Rams gave up on Dickson quickly and traded him to Dallas. The Cowboys didn't think much of him either and dumped him on the Cleveland Browns. The Browns were swiftly disenchanted, and Dickson went to the Vikings. So, two years and four teams later, Paul Dickson tried all over again to make good in pro football.

He was less than spectacular with Minnesota, and wasn't a sure-shot regular by any means. Then somebody got the idea that a player who stood 6 feet 5 inches tall and weighed 265 pounds might do better as a defensive lineman. And that was where he found his true niche. Marion Campbell, the Viking defensive line coach, took him in hand and showed him the moves. Intelligent, thoughtful, Dickson caught on quickly. He had the natural quickness needed by a defensive lineman, and his keen, mathematical brain read the offense pretty accurately. He continued to make mistakes, naturally. Most of the time he elected to gamble, to make the big play; it didn't always work out. But Dickson was also willing to work hard, to study ways of improving his play. And he began to make great progress.

During their first few years of play, the Viking defense was awful. At one time or another, it was last in almost all departments: most first downs allowed by rushing, most touchdowns allowed by rushing, most first downs allowed in a season, most total yardage allowed in a season. Yet the front four was really better than the statistics showed, especially taking into consideration that three-fourths of the defensive line consisted of Cleveland castoffs (Jim Prestel came to the Vikings from the Browns, just like Marshall and Dickson).

The way the team climbed in the standings those first three years was an indication that better things were in store. They were last in their division in 1961, the club's maiden season, with a 3–11–0 record. The following year they climbed to sixth; the won-lost record was 2–11–1, but that season the Los Angeles Rams were so bad that they shouldn't have been permitted on a pro football field, as their 1–12–1 record showed. In 1963 the Vikings went one notch higher, ahead of the Rams and 49ers. They had achieved a promising 5–8–1 record. They were scoring more points and their opponents were scoring fewer, and that is what they pay off on when the ballgame is over.

So, in three years the Vikings had won ten, lost thirty, tied two. And all signs pointed to further improvement when Minnesota drafted a bruiser of an all-American lineman named Carl Eller, who was already a local favorite, having played brilliantly for the University of Minnesota.

Had it not been for football, this 6-foot 6-inch bundle of muscles might have been a $100-a-week laborer in his home town of Winston-Salem, North Carolina. But he did play football, and he played well, and he was a sure-shot all-American even before he went to college. At least the University of Minnesota scouts thought so, because he had easily earned high school all-American honors. How could this huge but still growing boy fail to improve?

The scouts guessed right about Eller. As a sophomore, he was part of a fine Golden Gopher team, which journeyed to the Rose Bowl in 1962 and knocked off UCLA, 21–3. Eller's heroics during his college career brought him nationwide attention. In a game against the University of Michigan for the coveted Little Brown Jug, the Gophers were forced to punt. Eller was the first man downfield, and he hit the receiver so hard that the ball bounced loose. Minnesota recovered and went to a touchdown, the only one scored in the game. Against Wisconsin, Minnesota found itself pushed back to its own 1-yard line. The Badgers had possession, first and goal. But they didn't crack in, because Carl Eller personally barred the door. Eller senior year, Bubba Smith notwithstanding. The Rams were going to pick him, that much was certain. But Los Angeles also needed a running back and a wide receiver. Minnesota drafted judiciously. The Vikings made sure of getting Gene Washington and Clint Jones at the annual player selection, then dealt a running back, Tommy Mason, and a receiver, Hal Bedsole, to Los Angeles in exchange for Page. The trade began to pay off almost immediately.

Perhaps Page had heard too many stories about the size of pro football linemen. He probably reasoned that a little more heft would help him overpower the offensive blockers. Page reported to training camp hog-fat, tilting the scales at 275 pounds, roughly 20 pounds over his normal playing weight. Bud Grant took one look at his roly-poly rookie and raised the roof. Page took off the blubber in a hurry, and by the fourth game he broke into the starting lineup.

If the hopeful Minnesota fans expected miracles of the 1967 Vikings, they soon had to face reality. This team was going nowhere. In fact it won one game less than it had the previous season under Van Brocklin, posting a 3–8–3 record. Yet those who knew what to look for saw a great deal of improvement in spite of the won-lost figures.

The team had allowed 294 points, its lowest total ever. The defense looked a little sharper, tighter, and there was more spirit and discipline in this club. Also, the play of Alan Page indicated that perhaps better days were not too far away. A game against the Detroit Lions was the tipoff on Page.

Firing off the line almost in a frenzy, Page caused four fumbles and recovered one of them. With forty-five seconds left in the game, and the Lions driving, Minnesota tried frantically to protect the 10–10 tie. Page did it almost by himself. With the ball on the 20-yard line, he sifted through the blockers and nailed Tom Nowatzke, who fumbled as he was belted, and Minnesota recovered. But that day the whole Viking defense was charged up, and Detroit was forced into fumbles eleven times. For his magnificent effort, Page was named defensive player of the week.

The coaches, the players, and all the other knowledgeable people who followed the NFL also saw a couple of exciting tie games with Baltimore and Chicago. And in the Green Bay game, the Viking front four held Vince Lombardi's ball-control team to a puny forty-seven yards rushing while beating the Pack, 10–7. There was bound to be improvement the next year. And there was.

For this was a defensive line that was growing, maturing, solidifying, learning the tough business of playing up front. There wasn't a weak spot in it. Most important, these linemen knew how to play together, how to stunt and loop in around one another, how to put on the straight-ahead rush, how to work well with linebackers, how to pursue the ball carriers behind the line. It was a cohesive unit that opened the 1968 season.

The team went further than even the most diehard fans had hoped. Minnesota went into the Western Conference playoffs, and ran into an aroused Baltimore team, which did a hatchet job on them. But that's already been mentioned.

The year of destiny for the Minnesota Vikings was 1969. It didn't start out that way though. The upset by the Giants was hard to take, and for just that one week it seemed as if Bud Grant's boys were up to their old bad habits of blowing a lead, playing ragged football, taking it on the chin because of the bad breaks. But everything turned right-side-up after that. When the Vikings weren't good, they were lucky. And if you ask any athlete which he'd rather have, he'll tell you right off it's the breaks that count.

After the Giants debacle, the Baltimore Colts dropped in for a visit. This was the team that had almost run Minnesota out of town in the divisional playoff. The Vikings were out to get even.

Joe Kapp and his cutthroat offensive mob knocked the Colt

defense dizzy as Minnesota ran away and hid with the football. The score was 52–14, and Baltimore was never really in the game after the opening kickoff. The Eller-Page-Larsen-Marshall-Dickson unit gave the Colt passers no peace as they came busting in to force Unitas and Morrall into hurried passes. Carl Eller handled tackle Sam Ball in cavalier fashion, and Jim Marshall had almost no trouble with Bob Vogel on the line.

Next, the team from Green Bay came to town, and the Vikings were all ready for Bart Starr. Eight times Starr was dumped before he could get off a throw. Time after time the fast Green Bay running back, Travis Williams, was dropped for a loss, or held to a yard, two yards, maybe three. The Pack didn't get into Minnesota territory until the second half, and it managed to score a touchdown only in the final five seconds. The Packers got just 108 yards on the ground and 65 yards passing.

Against Chicago, Minnesota wasn't that good; but it was lucky. The first two Viking touchdowns were gifts, and one of those was an out-and-out freak. Just before the first period ended, Mike Reilly broke through and blocked a punt, which he also recovered in the end zone for a touchdown. Then, in the third period, Fred Cox attempted a field goal from the Chicago 47. The kick was blocked, but Cox plucked the football out of the air, took off, and ran 11 yards to the 29 for a first down. A few plays later, when it seemed that Chicago was holding, Joe Taylor was called for pass interference on Gene Washington. Kapp completed a pass from the 1-yard line, and the Vikings had a two-touchdown lead.

After that the Bears were trying to play catch-up football, but they couldn't get anywhere. The Viking front four rushed the quarterback constantly, so that the long bomb never went off. In fact, the Bear line did a commendable job on its own, flattening Joe Kapp five times. But Minnesota walked off the field with a 31–0 shutout.

Next came the Cardinals. St. Louis scored a touchdown on a pass interception and added a field goal. But the Vikings scored more often, and won, 27–10. The Cards were limited to seven first downs and a grand total of 169 yards passing and rushing.

Continuing their winning ways, Minnesota ravaged Detroit, 24–10. Greg Landry, Detroit's passer, was swamped six times. When he wasn't being sacked, Landry was throwing interceptions.

Then it was the Bears again, and Bobby Douglass was dropped nine times trying to get off passes. He lost seventy-eight yards trying to elude those monsters from Minnesota.

Cleveland was annihilated, 51–3. This was the team that had run amuck against Dallas the previous week, but against the Vikings they were helpless. The Browns' quarterbacks Bill Nelsen and Jerry Rhome, were pressured into four interceptions. Their running backs gained only forty-two yards.

Green Bay slowed the Vikings, but didn't stop them. The Vikings needed their share of luck to pull out the 9–7 squeaker. The Packers scored just once, on Doug Hart's eighty-five-yard return of an intercepted Joe Kapp throw. Twice Mike Mercer failed to kick a field goal for the Pack, once from only twenty-two yards out.

Pittsburgh fell, 52–14. That was the tenth game of the year, Minnesota had won nine of them. The Vikings had outscored the opposition, 319 points to 103. Some might say the offense was three times as good as the opposition; or that the defense was three times as good. It all depended on the point of view.

Minnesota won the Central Division title the following week, playing in the snow against the Detroit Lions. The team celebrated by making it a shutout victory, 27–0. It was a field day for all five members of the Viking line. Greg Landry was forced to eat the ball seven times in this return match, losing fifty-seven yards in the process. In the fourth quarter Alan

The Purple People Eaters

Page tipped Landry's pass, and Jim Marshall got the ball. Marshall galloped to the Detroit 12-yard line, and when Nick Eddy jumped on his back, Marshall flipped a lateral to Alan Page, who had started the whole thing. Page scored the touchdown.

The swing man, Paul Dickson, joined the fun by blocking a punt in the first quarter.

Everybody wondered what would happen when two standout front fours tangled, and they found out in the Viking-Rams game. Minnesota won, 20–13, but it was no cakewalk. The Norsemen never did get to Roman Gabriel, and the Fearsome Foursome of the Rams grabbed Kapp only once. Call it a near standoff in front-four effort.

After beating the 49ers to make it twelve in a row, Minnesota finally dropped one. The Falcons broke the streak. It wasn't that the Vikings weren't trying: they really wanted the victory, because their former coach, Norm Van Brocklin was at the Atlanta helm. Maybe the momentum wasn't there, maybe it was just that the game itself was meaningless in the standings. The Minnesota team offered no excuses.

The Vikings won the NFL crown that year with a 12–2–0 record. Many people gave most of the credit to tough Joe Kapp, the unorthodox passer with the heart of a tiger. Many more said it was the front four's personal victory. But neither Kapp nor the Purple People Eaters had occasion to boast after the final contest of the season—the Super Bowl game against Kansas City.

The No-Nickname Line

OF ALL THE TEAM SPORTS ENGAGED IN BY the strong young men of America, the game of football has changed the most over the years. And not merely in the rules. Every sport is tinkered with sporadically in that department, and most of the time the changes aren't drastic. When the guardians of baseball felt that the pitcher should take less time between pitches, nobody seemed to mind much; in fact, the new rule has seldom been enforced.

Once in a while a sport other than football may make a big change. For example, the year basketball eliminated the center jump after a basket had been scored, the philosophy and strategy of the game changed. But after that it remained the same for a long time. Maybe it was because no new concept was possible.

Not so with football. Perhaps it's because the game lends itself so readily to constant change, even when no new rule of importance has been added. There are still only eleven men on a side, and the field's dimensions haven't changed (except for professional football's positioning of the goal posts on the goal line). Yet the brand of football of the 1970's is almost totally different from that of only a quarter of a century before. And it is because there have been such men as Tom Landry and Vince Lombardi and George Halas and Hank Stram, who dope out new wrinkles on offense or defense. These wrinkles lead to others, and before the fans know what's happening, the face of the game has altered.

Usually, the offense has begun the changes. The T formation had led to a five-man line. The third end resulted in the 4–3 alignment. The experiments that followed, initiated by Landry and Stram, began to have their own repercussions. There were a lot of defensive headaches hidden in the new-fangled multiple offense, which featured I formations, double flankers, slotbacks stationed between guard and tackle, and a new passing scheme, developed by Stram, which he dubbed the "movable pocket."

Oddly enough, the very men who invented the offensive gimmicks also invented the antidotes, partly because other teams were wise enough to experiment with the new offensive formations too.

For example, Stram—and probably one or two other coaches —dreamed up a defensive setup that he called "the Stack" (others gave it different names, such as "Oklahoma"). This setup turned the 4–3 into a 3–4. Like all formations, it had certain built-in advantages and disadvantages.

Its effectiveness lay in the fact that many times a big defensive tackle lined up against a usually smaller offensive center whom he could blow through. Variations in spacing made it difficult for offensive blockers to execute their assignments. Receivers moving out for short look-in passes found themselves in a crowd. And, with all its shifting around, the Stack caused quarterbacks to call more audibles at the line of scrimmage than was really safe.

As for drawbacks, the Stack was more easily suckered into trap plays. There wasn't as much pressure in a rush at the quarterback. And it was complicated to learn! Refinements in the 4–3 had been difficult enough to absorb, but this? Didn't the defense have enough to worry about without all these gymnastics?

So, as the 1960's came to a close, the multiple offense and the Stack and other exotic tidbits were merely looming large in the future. "Football of the 1970's" some coaches called it. Mostly, they stuck with the 4–3, and a few special variations thrown in when necessary. And one of the best front fours of the late 1960's played for the Kansas City Chiefs.

For, although Hank Stram liked to tinker with the X and the O, and make arrows shoot out in all directions, he was still enough of a traditionalist to realize that the front four was the tried-and-tested grouping, the bread-and-butter defense, the solid line of forward fortifications. He also knew that the road to championships was paved by great defenses, and since he had won two American Football League title games before the two professional leagues were merged, Stram evidently knew how to construct a solid line of breastworks.

On January 15, 1967, Kansas City became the first American League team to confront a National League team in the Super Bowl. That was Stram's third AFL championship team, and he thought it was a good one. It was. But he had the misfortune to meet a Green Bay team that was one of Vince Lombardi's better aggregations (none of them was really bad). Yet, for half a game, he stayed right up there with the mighty Pack. After all, the short end of a 14–10 score is nothing that can't be overcome by one bomb, one break-away run, one bit of luck.

In the third quarter, one wrong swing of Len Dawson's arm turned the game into a Green Bay breeze. On third-and-5, Green Bay served up the blitz. Dawson, rushed, barely got the ball away. It floated soft and short, right into the arms of a defensive back, Willie Wood, who ran the ball back to the Kansas City 5-yard line. Elijah Pitts scored on the next play, and it was bye-bye ballgame. Nothing the defense or offense could do worked after that.

Sick at heart over their poor showing, the Kansas City Chiefs picked up the pieces and went home, hoping mightily for another chance at the cream of the NFL. They weren't as bad as the 35–10 score seemed to indicate. One interception had killed them. But maybe next time things would be different.

But they had to wait three years for the opportunity to present itself, and in the meantime there were regular season games to be played, vacancies to fill, strategies to devise. The front four had to be looked over. For the most part it was as solid as any in pro football. But any section of a team can be improved. This line didn't need too much in the way of added strength.

The veteran of the four was 6-foot 4-inch, 250-pound Jerry Mays at end. A fifth draft choice from Southern Methodist University, Mays had come up in 1951, when the Kansas City Chiefs were operating as the Dallas Texans.

Mays was a tackle in college, but had little difficulty making the transition to end. In fact that position suited him much better. Most defensive tackles are stronger than ends, and Mays, although no weakling, was noted more for hustle and desire than for power. Coupled with good moves and a lot of experience, that made him one of the best in the league.

Ever since boyhood Mays had hero-worshipped SMU football players. When he was a halfback in high school, his attention was centered on Kyle Rote and Doak Walker, and everyone knows how good they were. When he became a lineman at SMU, those idols didn't seem to fit, so he tried to pattern himself after another line star, Forrest Gregg of the Packers. In that first Super Bowl game, Mays found himself opposite Jerry Kramer and the very same Forrest Gregg, which was usually enough to bother any defensive lineman. Just before

Green Bay scored its final touchdown, Kramer turned to Gregg and said, "Old buddy, I'll block out Andy Rice and you get the guy whose idol you are." That's what happened, too. Those Packers sure knew how to hurt a guy!

At tackle was an immovable object named Junius "Buck" Buchanan, probably the most vicious tackler in the AFL. Standing 6 feet 7 inches and weighing close to 290, Buck was usually double-teamed, because one man trying to stop him might be knocked loose from his uniform.

Buchanan's introduction to college football at Grambling College was something of a shocker. He wasn't quite so heavy then, and in his first scrimmage he was sent up against a chap named Ernie Ladd, who towered 6 feet 9 inches and tipped the scales at 300 pounds. Buck heard the quarterback holler "hut-hut-hut"—and the next thing he knew, he was flat on his back.

Little Grambling was a veritable athletic factory that year. Walking around the campus were Lane Howell, Garland Boyette, Clifton McNeil, Willie Williams, and Ladd, all of whom played pro football later. Willis Reed was on the basketball team, and Tommie Agee played some baseball. What other college in the United States of America ever had so much talent present at the same time?

In spite of his size, Buchanan was stunningly fast on his feet, especially on a straight-away run. He was clocked at 4.9 seconds in the forty-yard dash, which was actually linebacker speed. Buck joined the Chiefs in 1963.

In 1966 a gritty all-American from the University of Minnesota arrived. His name was Aaron Brown, and he stood up tall at 6 feet 5 inches; he was also pretty hefty, packing around 260 pounds. Brown was so versatile that at first Stram didn't know what to do with him.

In college, Brown had played fullback and tight end, as well as some defensive football. He was also a standout receiver.

Playing against Ohio State, he caught six passes, and then against Northwestern he made eight grabs. He was also the fastest man on the Minnesota team. Naturally, Stram figured that he had a fine fullback on his hands, one who could run with the ball, catch it, and also block like fury. Possibly he envisioned Brown and Mike Garrett as a unit in the backfield, and that combination would be tough to stop. However, the pairing was only a wistful dream. Brown started only one game in 1966; he came down with a calcified muscle in his leg and missed the rest of the season. When he returned, it was as a defensive end.

Probably the best example of Brown's defensive capability showed up in a 1968 game against Houston. The Oilers had the ball on the Kansas City 13-yard line, and Pete Beathard moved into the pocket for a pass. Only he never did get to throw the ball. For Brown went barreling in, stripped off the blockers like the skin off a banana, and started to chase the terrified quarterback. Back went Beathard, with Brown after him—back, back, back—until the Kansas City lineman caught his man and fell on him. The play lost twenty-five yards!

The fourth man should have been huge Ernie Ladd, and actually he did play for the Chiefs, after having been obtained in a trade. But Ladd was hurting then, his legs were giving out, and the old desire was gone. Stram needed someone else. And he found him: Curley Culp, a 6-foot 1-inch, 265-pound bundle of dynamite.

They called Culp "The Puma from Yuma" at his alma mater, Arizona State University. Not only was he a great lineman, but he was also a champion wrestler, NCAA champ in 1968 and an alternate on the Olympic team that year. He earned his muscles tossing around 50-pound barrels on his father's hog farm. Curley was drafted in 1968 by the Denver Broncos, but he never made the team. It's hard to say why. Maybe it was because the head coach thought he might work out better as an offensive lineman. But Culp had never played offense; he was a man who had to use his hands and throw people around, just like those barrels back on the farm. Denver placed him on the waiver list, hoping nobody else would want him so that he could be placed on the taxi squad. Paul Brown, head coach of the Cincinnati Bengals, put in a claim right away, and Culp was taken off the list. Finally, Curley was put on the block again. Hank Stram gladly took him in and gave him a home in the Kansas City front four. Curley fit in like a well-worn easy chair.

The Chiefs ended the 1968 season with five straight victories, and they opened the 1969 calendar with a pair of easy wins: 27–9 over San Diego and 31–0 against Boston. The defense looked sharp, tight. In two games it had yielded one field goal and one touchdown. Local sportswriters began casting around for a proper nickname to hang on the front four. Most of the good ones already seemed to have been taken: "Fearsome Foursome," "Four Norsemen," "Purple People Eaters," "Doomsday Defense," and the like. After a while they decided to let well enough alone. Let this quartet be known as the "No-Nickname" Foursome.

Overconfidence can be as bad as a fumble or an interception, and the Chiefs found that out when lowly Cincinnati beat them, 24–19. Gone was the seven-game winning streak. True, they could find a good reason for losing if they had to. Len Dawson had hurt his knee and didn't play in the game. Jacky Lee was rusty. But professionals don't try to alibi. A loss is a loss, and that's the end of it.

The test of a champion is the ability to get off the floor and come back. That the Chiefs did. They reeled off another chain of seven, including a shutout over Houston and a fine effort against San Diego, in which the Chargers were held to a field goal, no more. During the streak the Chiefs also made sure to teach Cincinnati a 42–22 lesson, and they handled Joe Namath's crowd of New York Jets in fine style with a 34–16 win. The streak lifted them back to an even status with Oakland, which had also suffered an upset at the hands of Cincinnati, after having won fifteen games in a row.

The eleventh game of the season matched the two contenders, Oakland and Kansas City. And the Chiefs blew it. That is, the offense did. The Raiders scored three touchdowns, but two of them came on pass interceptions, one going twenty-two yards, and the other seventy-five.

Still the Chiefs weren't out of it. There were three games left on the schedule, with the finale against the Raiders. If Kansas City could win them all, they'd be home free, and take the Western Division title.

The Chiefs went to work and wrecked Denver, 31–17. The score was misleading—the Broncos didn't score their two touchdowns until the Chiefs had the game in the bag.

Buffalo gave them a lot more trouble, but still they came through. The Bills, with the great O. J. Simpson in the lineup, were fighting for second place in the East, so they had a lot going for them. Simpson was particularly rough, helping himself to a thirty-two-yard touchdown run. But the Mays-Culp-Buchanan-Brown combination was equal to the task.

But when it came down to the nitty-gritty, when the season seemed to hinge on one all-or-nothing victory, Kansas City failed. Oakland won the wrapup and the divisional title, 10–6. It was then that the sportswriters hung a bum rap on the Chiefs. Stram's club, they said, couldn't win the *must* games. They folded under pressure. How little they knew!

For, in this final year before the complete merger of the two leagues, there was a complicated system of playoffs worked out. The divisional champions had to play two games, not one, and the winner of both would make the trip to the Super Bowl. In a way it was only fair, because the NFL had four divisions and the winners had to play one another. The AFL had only two. Therefore, the Eastern Division champs, New York, played

Kansas City, while the Western Division leader, Oakland, played the Eastern runner-up, Houston. And winner takes all in the AFL.

Picking strictly on form, Kansas City looked like a better bet than New York in all the vital statistics. The Chiefs had won one game more than the Jets. They had scored six points more than Joe Namath and company. Also, in defense there was just no comparison. For Kansas City led the league in that department, having given up only 177 points in fourteen games. Only one team in the NFL had a better defensive record, and that was Minnesota, the Purple People Eaters, who allowed 133 points all year, or 9.5 per game.

Those who were guided by form would have guessed right. The Chiefs and Jets slugged it out, and Kansas City won, 13–6.

Meanwhile, Oakland did everything but chase Houston out of the stadium. That score was 56–7.

So it was Oakland against Kansas City once more, both with good defensive clubs. In fact, the Raiders were second only to the Chiefs in defense, but for different reasons. Whereas the Chiefs' strongest point was in the line, Oakland's was in the deep secondary. The two cornerbacks and two safety men were sometimes called "the soul patrol," and they zoomed around the atmosphere knocking down and intercepting passes all the livelong day. And their line, featuring Ike Lassiter and ungentle Ben Davidson at ends, wasn't exactly a pushover either.

Oakland scored first toward the close of the first quarter, and then held Kansas City in check until near the end of the half. The No-Nickname four wasn't doing much to help out, and the offense was doing practically nothing at all. In fact, the Chiefs didn't get into Oakland territory until a minute or so before the half ended, but when they did, they scored. Most of the work came about on a forty-one-yard pass to Otis Taylor.

The Chiefs took heart then. They had been badly outplayed, yet the score was tied. Fearful until this point of falling behind by a bigger score than 7–0, the Kansas City four had had to play it close to the vest. Now they could resume normal operations, meaning cream the passer when possible. This they proceeded to do.

There was no fancy stuff by the No-Nickname quartet in the second half, simply straight-ahead power. They cracked in on Daryle Lamonica and almost broke the quarterback in half. Three times he was reached by Aaron Brown, and one of those times was the end of the ballgame for all practical purposes. As Brown ripped in with lowered head, Lamonica was just letting go of the ball. His arm described a sweeping arc, and on the follow through, his thumb and first two fingers jammed against Brown's face mask. The passer strained a tendon in his pitching hand and he walked off the field in great pain.

In came George Blanda, the old man of the mountain. He got nowhere. He missed on two straight plays, one a pass and the other a field-goal attempt. When Oakland got the ball again, Blanda did all right for a while, then threw an interception. Kansas City was off and running. Ten plays later the Chiefs were in the Raider end zone.

Oakland never did get back into the ballgame. But Len Dawson and his running backs didn't do too well either. Actually, it seemed as though each team thought of the game as a hot potato and tried to give it to the other, only neither one could hold on to it long enough. Kansas City fumbled three times and Lamonica, playing with sore hand and all, was intercepted three times.

How good was the Kansas City front four? Very good indeed. It was they who won the game. They were simply magnificent against the running game, and the second-half pressure they exerted against the Oakland passers was fearful to behold. Some statistics:

Oakland ran off seventy-seven plays (to Kansas City's fifty-seven). Their four running backs gained seventy-nine yards in twenty-eight carries for an average of 2.8 per carry. No run was longer than nine yards, and there were only two of those. The passers were dropped four times for a combined loss of thirty-seven yards. Mays-Culp-Brown-Buchanan had done a commendable day's work.

So Minnesota and Kansas City, the two best defensive teams in professional football, did get the desired matchup. Because of a superior all-around record, the Vikings were two-touchdown favorites. But everybody watching the game—and that included about fifty or sixty million fans seated before television sets—knew that the game would be decided up front.

Minnesota took the kickoff, made a couple of first downs and had to punt. Most of the yardage was picked up by Joe Kapp's passes as Dave Osborne and Bill Brown found the going tough. Three cracks into the line netted a meager 6 yards.

Kansas City did somewhat better, but not on the ground. Dawson hit for a pair of first downs, but nowhere enough yardage to cause concern. The trouble started when Jan Stenerud came in to try for a field goal from the Viking 48-yard line.

What might have seemed strange to those who tuned in late and didn't hear about field conditions was the fact that Minnesota had marched to the Chiefs 39, and then punted. Yet there was Stenerud making the attempt from 9 yards farther out.

The answer lay in the 15-mile-an-hour wind favoring the Chiefs. Fred Cox was pretty good with the square-toed shoe, and had he been in Stenerud's position, possibly he too would have made it.

At any rate Stenerud did boot it true, and Kansas City had a 3-point edge.

Once again the Kansas City four asserted itself. Curley Culp got Bill Brown after a 3-yard gain, and then Mays sacked Kapp for a loss of 6. An end sweep by Brown got back 10, but not enough for the first down. However, Minnesota retained possession when Kansas City was hit with a roughing-the-

The No-Nickname Line

kicker penalty. But that didn't do much good. Because of the tremendous rush put on by the Chiefs' line, Kapp had to throw short. Three completions got only 8 yards.

The Viking line was also living up to its press notices. The enemy ground attack wasn't effective, and the Minnesota defense was giving Dawson a hard time, forcing him to throw under duress. Kansas City got another field goal only because of a pass-interference penalty called on Ed Sharockman, Minnesota's right cornerback.

Like a Chinese water torture, the Chiefs kept pecking away with field goals. Stenerud got his third one midway in the second period, and this time it *was* the fault of one of the Four Norsemen.

Dawson noticed that Carl Eller at left end kept pinching in sharply. The way Eller moved, he could stop a standard end sweep by a running back, or at least knock over some of the blockers. But he was coming in too sharply for another type of end run. So, with the ball on Minnesota's 44, Dawson called for an end-around, with the wide receiver Frank Pitts, who was split out to the left, taking the ball and sweeping deep and laterally around Eller's flank to the right. It worked for 19 yards!

Thoroughly ashamed of themselves for getting hooked on a simple sucker play, Minnesota's four dug in and stopped the opposition cold. But Stenerud had his way anyhow.

And then, suddenly, the game broke wide open! Charlie West fumbled the kickoff and Kansas City recovered. Frantically, the Vikings dug in on their own 19.

Jim Marshall drove through and dropped Dawson for a loss of 8. Sensing another pass, the Vikings blitzed again. But Dawson crossed them with a draw, and Hayes carried for 13. Then Dawson passed to Otis Taylor on the 4. Garrett lost a yard and Dawson was held for no gain. On third down little Mike Garrett went over left guard for the touchdown.

The game wasn't over by a long shot, and Minnesota did

strike back early in the third period, when the fuming Joe Kapp led the club on a 10-play, 69-yard touchdown march to make the score 16–7. But Kansas City got that one back, helped by one key play.

The Chiefs were on their own 32, third-and-7 in the third quarter. If they failed, they'd have to kick. Buoyed by a strong defensive stand, the Vikings might pick up momentum and start moving. A 9-point spread was far from being safe.

Dawson saw that Eller was up to his old tricks again, coming in on a straight slant, probably to get in on the passer quicker. Well, why not? Third-and-7, deep in their own territory, that certainly was a passing situation. Only Dawson didn't pass. He dug out the Frank Pitts end-around again, and it carried for 7 yards and the crucial first down. Two plays later, Dawson hit Otis Taylor with a quick one. Taylor broke two tackles and scampered all the way home. That was the crusher!

The Vikings went through the motions, but they were doomed. The coup de grace was administered about 5 minutes before time ran out. Never-quit Joe Kapp dropped back to pass, and Aaron Brown chased him back 13 yards before clobbering him. Kapp got up holding his right arm and walked slowly off the field, head down, almost weeping with rage and frustration. Gary Cuozzo took over, and three plays later he threw an interception. Dawson took possession and ran out the clock. The final score was 23–7.

Statistically, the Kansas City front four came out slightly ahead of the Four Norsemen. Buck Buchanan and his playmates permitted only two first downs rushing and 67 yards on the ground, while the Chiefs picked up eight first downs and 151 yards on rushing plays. Both sides got to the quarterback three times; the Chiefs lost 20 yards, the Vikings 27. Minnesota had a passing edge, 172 yards to 122—but those were offensive statistics.

Before the game, Hank Stram made a little speech about the state of modern football. He said:

"The decade of the '60's was the decade of simplicity. The good teams—the Green Bay Packers for example—came out almost all the time in the same set and ran the play. In effect, what they said was, here we come, see if you can stop us.

"The '70's will be the decade of difference—different offensive sets, different defensive formations. . . ."

Maybe so. But not so that anyone would notice it from the Minnesota-Kansas City game. For the defenses were nearly always 4-3, with only some few variations from time to time.

And when the chips were down, when the Chiefs desperately needed to keep a drive going, they called on the end-around, which is a kissin' cousin to the old Statue of Liberty play, and that kind of stuff went out with bathtub gin and the Charleston.

Perhaps the 1970's will see something new, different, exciting. Football has a way of coming up with the unexpected, the original. But until it does, those coaches who set great store by the basic fundamentals of the game will stick to the 4-3—those four no-longer-unsung heroes of the defensive line.

Appendix:

OFFICIAL PLAY-BY-PLAY
DETROIT LIONS vs. GREEN BAY PACKERS
TIGER STADIUM, NOVEMBER 22, 1962, 12 NOON

WEATHER: CLOUDY; TEMPERATURE: 35°; WIND: WNW at 20 MPH;

Detroit won the toss and elected to receive. Green Bay chose to defend the north goal. Detroit sent Studstill and Watkins deep to receive. Kramer kicked off to Watkins on the 10, and he returned 10 yards to the 29.

Yard Line Code:
L—Lions
P—Packers

Note: All line positions refer to *offensive* team.

LIONS

1–10–29L	Lewis hit right tackle for *two* yards.
2–8–31L	Lewis slipped at left tackle and lost a yard.
3–9–30L	*Plum passed to Cogdill for 19 yards and a first down.*
1–10–49L	Lewis ran wide around right end for *two* yards to the Packer 49.
2–8–49P	Plum's pass intended for Pietrosante was incomplete.
3–8–49P	*Plum passed to Studstill for 17 yards and a first down.*
1–10–32P	Lewis got *two* yards at right guard, where he fumbled and Gremminger recovered on the 17.

135

PACKERS

1–10–17P	Starr's pass intended for McGee was incomplete.
2–10–17P	*Starr passed to McGee for 26 yards and a first down.*
1–10–43P	Taylor tried left end and picked up *four* yards.
2–6–47P	Karras broke through to drop Moore for a *three*-yard loss.
3–9–44P	McCord, Karras, and Schmidt dropped Starr for a loss, but Green Bay was penalized *five* yards for delay.
3–14–39P	Brown dropped Starr for a 15-yard loss.
4–29–24P	Dowler punted out of bounds on the Packer 39 (15-yard punt).

LIONS

1–10–39P	Lewis got *three* yards at left tackle.
2–7–36P	Pietrosante got *three* on the draw.
3–4–33P	*Plum passed to Cogdill for 33 yards, a first down and a touchdown.*

DETROIT 6	GREEN BAY 0	Time: 8:28. The drive covered 39 yards in 3 plays.
Walker converted		
DETROIT 7	GREEN BAY 0	

6:32. Walker kicked off to Adderley on the 21. No return.

PACKERS

1–10–21P	Moore tried right guard and managed a yard to the 22.
2–9–22P	*Moore ran wide around left end for 17 yards and a first down.*
1–10–39P	A whole host of Lions dropped Starr for a *nine*-yard loss.
2–19–30P	Starr ran around right end for *five* yards.
3–14–35P	Williams dropped Taylor for a *one*-yard loss at center.
4–15–34P	Dowler's punt was partially blocked by Scholtz and rolled dead on the Lion 44.

LIONS

1–10–44L	Lewis picked up *four* yards at right tackle, fumbled, and Green Bay recovered on the 48.

PACKERS

1–10–48L	Moore got a yard at center and fumbled. Brettschneider recovered for Detroit on the Lion 46.

Official Play-by-Play

LIONS

1-10-46L Watkins got *five* yards at right tackle.
2-5-49P   *Watkins got 11 yards at right end for a first down.*
1-10-38P *Webb got 14 yards and a first down at right tackle.*
1-10-24P The quarter ended before another play could get under way.

FIRST-QUARTER SCORE: DETROIT 7   GREEN BAY 0

SECOND QUARTER

LIONS

1-10-24P Watkins tried left end and lost *three* to the 27.
2-13-27P Plum's pass intended for Studstill at the goal line was thrown short; incomplete.
3-13-27P *Plum passed to Cogdill for 27 yards, a first down and a touchdown.*

DETROIT 13   GREEN BAY 0   Time: 0:58. The drive covered 54 yards in
Walker converted   *six* plays.
DETROIT 14   GREEN BAY 0

Walker kicked off to Adderley *six* yards deep, and he returned 27 yards to the 21.

PACKERS

1-10-21P Brettschneider batted down a Starr pass at the line.
2-10-21P *Brown broke through and caused Starr to fumble on the six, where Williams picked it up and waltzed into the end zone for a 6-yard touchdown.*

DETROIT 20   GREEN BAY 0   Time: 1:19. The
Walker converted   drive covered
DETROIT 21   GREEN BAY 0   *six* yards.

Walker kicked off to Adderley on the 3; he fumbled and recovered his own fumble on the 10 (7-yard return).

PACKERS

1-10-10P Taylor was dropped for a *six*-yard loss by Brown.

Official Play-by-Play

2–16–4P   Moore got *three* yards at right guard.
3–13–7P   *Brown dropped Starr in the end zone for a safety.*

    DETROIT 23   GREEN BAY 0   TIME: 3:16.

Dowler free-kicked to Cogdill on the 45, and he returned 4 yards.

Detroit was penalized 15 yards back to the 34.

LIONS

1–10–34L   Watkins got 3 yards at right tackle.
2–7–37L   *Webb ran around right end for 12 yards and a first down.*
1–10–49L   10:18. *Webb ran up the middle for 12 yards and a first down.*
1–10–39P   Watkins picked up 2 yards at left guard.
2–8–37P   Lewis got 4 at left tackle.
3–4–33P   Plum passed complete to Gibbons for *two* yards.
4–2–31P   Plum's field goal attempt was blocked by Quinlan. No return at the 39.

PACKERS

1–10–39P   Starr was dropped for a 9-yard loss by Walker.
2–19–30P   Starr's pass was caught beautifully by Dowler for 13 yards.
3–6–43P   Taylor lost *two* yards at center on the draw play.
4–8–41P   McGee punted to Studstill on the 22, and he returned 31 yards to the Packer 47. Offsetting penalties nullified the play, and the officials placed the ball on the 45.

Green Bay was allowed to kick over and elected to run. *McGee, back to punt, ran around right end for eight yards and a first down.*

1–10–47L   Taylor hit left tackle for no gain.
2–10–47L   McCord dropped Starr for a *nine*-yard loss.
3–19–44P   Starr passed to Kramer for 19 yards, short of a first down.
4–1–37L   Taylor tried right guard for no gain.

LIONS

1–10–37L   Webb lost *two* yards at left end.
2–12–35L   Plum passed to Watkins for *seven* yards.
3–5–42L   2:00 left. Detroit drew *five* yards for illegal procedure.

Official Play-by-Play

3–10–37L	Plum's pass intended for Studstill was overthrown; incomplete.
4–10–37L	1:54. Detroit drew *five* yards for delay.
4–15–32L	Lary punted into the end zone (63-yard punt).

PACKERS

1–10–20P	Karras dropped Starr for a *nine*-yard loss.
2–19–11P	Starr's pass intended for McGee was incomplete.
3–19–11P	1:17. Karras dropped Starr for a *six*-yard loss.
4–25–5P	Lane was called for roughing the kicker, and Green Bay received a first down by penalty.
1–10–20P	*Starr passed to Kramer for 11 yards and a first down.*
1–10–31P	*Starr passed to Dowler for 10 yards and a first down.*
1–10–41P	0:45. *Starr passed to Dowler for 13 yards and a first down.*
1–10–46L	*Starr passed to Kramer for 20 yards and a first down.*
1–10–26L	Starr passed to Moore for 2 yards.
2–8–24L	Kramer's field goal attempt was blocked by Brown and picked up on the Lion 14 by Lowe and returned 28 yards to the 42 as the half ended.

HALFTIME SCORE: DETROIT 23   GREEN BAY 0

THIRD QUARTER

Walker kicked off to Moore on the six, and he returned 26 yards to the 32.

PACKERS

1–10–32P	Moore tried left tackle and got *two* yards.
2–8–34P	Starr's pass intended for Dowler was intercepted on the Lion 40 by Lane and returned two yards.

LIONS

1–10–42L	Watkins was dropped for a *one*-yard loss in the backfield.
2–11–41L	*Plum passed to Gibbons for 14 yards and a first down.*
1–10–45P	Webb ran up the middle for *five* yards to the 40.
2–5–40P	Plum's pass intended for Gibbons was thrown too low; incomplete.

140 *Official Play-by-Play*

3–5–40P   Watkins ran around left end and was dropped for no gain.
4–5–40P   *Plum kicked a 47-yard field goal at 3:39.*

DETROIT 26   GREEN BAY 0

Walker kicked off to Adderley in the end zone, where it was downed.

PACKERS

1–10–20P   Moore tried left guard and hit a wall for no gain.
2–10–20P   Schmidt broke through to drop Starr for a 15-yard loss on the 5.
3–25–5P   Taylor ran around right end for *five* yards.
4–20–10P   McGee punted dead on the Lion 45.

LIONS

1–10–45L   Watkins hit left guard for 5 yards.
2–5–50   8:33. Watkins lost a yard on a reverse around right end.
3–6–49L   *Plum passed to Studstill for 18 yards and a first down.*
1–10–33P   Webb got *three* yards at right end.
2–7–30P   Plum's pass intended for Watkins was intercepted by Whittenton on the 12, and he returned 36 yards to the Packer 48.

PACKERS

1–10–48P   Moore was dropped for a *two*-yard loss by Karras.
2–12–46P   Starr ran around right end for *five* yards to the Lion 49.
3–7–49L   About half of the Lion team dropped Starr for a 10-yard loss.
4–17–41P   McGee punted out of bounds on the Lion 36.

LIONS

1–10–36L   4:06. Plum's long pass intended for Studstill was incomplete.
2–10–36L   *Watkins ran wide around right end for 10 yards and a first down.*
1–10–46L   Webb broke over right tackle for *nine* yards at the Packer 45.
2–1–45P   *Plum ran around right end for 12 yards and a first down.*
1–10–33P   *Watkins ran inside left end for 13 yards and a first down.*
1–10–20P   2:25. Webb cut inside right tackle for *six* yards to the 14.
2–4–14P   Nitschke dropped Watkins for a *three*-yard loss.

Official Play-by-Play

3–7–17P   Plum's pass intended for Webb was thrown too low; incomplete.

4–7–17P   Plum's field goal attempt from the 24 was blocked by Adderley at the 31.

PACKERS

1–10–31P   Moore got *four* at right guard as the quarter ended.

THIRD-QUARTER SCORE: DETROIT 26   GREEN BAY 0

FOURTH QUARTER

PACKERS

2–6–35P   Taylor got 15 yards at right guard, fumbled, and Lary recovered at the Lion 42.

LIONS

1–10–42L   Watkins got *one* yard at right end, but Detroit was penalized 15 yards for holding.

1–25–28L   Watkins got no gain at right tackle.

2–25–28L   *Plum's pass was intercepted by Quinlan on the 4, and he ran it into the end zone, where he fumbled. Davis recovered for a touchdown.*

DETROIT 26   GREEN BAY 6
                 Kramer converted   Time: 1:26.
DETROIT 26   GREEN BAY 7

Kramer kicked off to Studstill on the 10, and he returned to the 20.

Green Bay was penalized 15 yards for face-mask foul.

DETROIT

1–10–35L   Webb got *two* at right end.

2–8–37L   13:00. Watkins tried left guard and picked up a yard.

3–7–38L   Morrall passed to Webb for *two* yards to the 40.

4–5–40L   Lary punted to Wood on the 24, and he returned 29 yards to the Lion 47.

Official Play-by-Play

PACKERS

1–10–47L	Starr passed to Dowler for *five* yards to the 42.
2–5–42L	*Taylor ran around right end for 20 yards and a first down.*
1–10–22L	LeBeau intercepted a Starr pass on the 17, and he returned 6 yards.

LIONS

1–10–23L	Webb got 2 yards at left guard.
2–8–25L	Webb tried right end and lost *one* yard.
3–9–24L	Morrall passed to Gibbons for 8 yards.
4–1–32L	Lary punted to the 35, where it touched Kostelnik and he fell on it.

PACKERS

1–10–35P	Starr's pass intended for Dowler was incomplete.
2–10–35P	*Starr passed to McGee for 11 yards and a first down.*
1–10–46P	Starr's pass intended for Kramer was incomplete.
2–10–46P	6:39. Starr's pass intended for Taylor was incomplete.
3–10–46P	Taylor carried around left end for *five* yards to the Lion 49.
4–5–49L	Green Bay drew *five* yards for offside.
4–10–46P	McGee punted out of bounds on the Lion 14.

LIONS

1–10–14L	5:25. Morrall fumbled, and Davis recovered on the 14.

PACKERS

1–10–14L	Brown dropped Starr for a *five*-yard loss on the 19.
2–15–19L	Starr passed complete to Kramer for 12 yards.
3–3–7L	Moore got *two* yards at left guard.
4–1–5L	*Taylor got one yard and a first down at center.*
1–4–4L	*Taylor ran over left guard for four yards and a touchdown.*

DETROIT 26	GREEN BAY 13	Time: 12:29. The
	Kramer converted	drive covered 14
DETROIT 26	GREEN BAY 14	yards in *five* plays.

Wood kicked off to Hall on the 44. No return.

LIONS

1–10–44L	Watkins ran around right end for *six* yards to the 50.
2–4–50	2:00 left. Watkins ran up the middle for three yards.
3–1–47P	*Watkins ran around right end for 4 yards and a first down.*
1–10–43P	Detroit was penalized *five* yards for delay.
1–15–48P	0:26. Morrall got *four* yards on a sneak. (Packer time out—4 sec.)
2–11–44P	Morrall got *five* yards on a keeper as the game ended.

FINAL SCORE: DETROIT 26   GREEN BAY 14

Official attendance: 57,598 (Largest Thanksgiving Day crowd and second largest all-time Lion home crowd)

HOWARD LISS began writing at the age of sixteen—for radio. Before he tried his hand at books he wrote for Broadway, television, and comic strips, including five years with *Buck Rogers*. Of his more than thirty books, most are about sports —*AFL Dream Backfield*, *Playoff!*, *The Making of a Rookie*. Mr. Liss collaborated on *Yogi Berra's Baseball Guidebook*, Y. A. Tittle's *Pro Quarterback*, Willie Mays's *My Secrets of Baseball*, and "Curly" Morrison's *The Strategy of Pro Football*.

When he is not traveling with a team, Howard Liss lives and works in New York.

U—one covering eighty-three yards—to set an NFL record of 214 touchdown passes in a lifetime. And of course he was to throw many more later.

The following week the Vikings squandered leads twice to allow Dallas to sneak out with a 28–17 victory.

The 32–31 loss to Detroit was bile-bitter. The Lions hadn't won a game all season, but they beat the Vikings because their field-goal kicker, a 5-foot 8-inch, 160-pound lad named Garo Yepremian (he had no college experience before coming to the pros) kicked six field goals in eight tries.

Minnesota must have been talking to the four winds in rage after a 20–13 upset loss to floundering Atlanta. The Falcons scored one touchdown on a sixty-two-yard return of an intercepted pass and another when they recovered a fumble on the Viking 1-yard line.

The final game of the season showed how one player with a hot hand can grind up even the best defense—which the Vikings certainly didn't have. The man was Gale Sayers of the Chicago Bears, and he showed Minnesota who was boss from the opening kickoff, which he ran back ninety yards for a touchdown. In that game Sayers accounted for 339 yards, by returning kicks, rushing, and receiving.

There had been rumors of dissension on the 1966 team, and that may have been true, for in February of the next year the head coach, Norm Van Brocklin, resigned. He was replaced by Bud Grant, who had been head coach of the Winnipeg Blue Bombers in the Canadian League. The same year, Alan Page joined the Vikings fresh from Notre Dame.

The State of Minnesota wanted Alan Page even before he began playing college football. Murray Warmath, the University of Minnesota coach, saw Page play high school football in Canton, Ohio, and called him the best high school lineman he had ever seen. But Page chose Notre Dame, with mixed results. He was pretty good as a sophomore, pretty terrible as a junior, and probably the best lineman in college football during his had been a fine prospect as a sophomore and won some all-America mention as a junior. In his senior year he was *everybody's* all-American.

The 1964 Vikings were the best yet. They ended in a second-place tie with Green Bay, both teams ringing up an 8–5–1 season. Actually, the Viking offense had also improved, and the team scored more points than Green Bay. But the great Packer defense allowed fewer points.

Gary Larsen came to the Vikings the following year from the Rams, who had made him tenth draft choice the year before. He was the only member of the Viking defensive line who hadn't played at a big school. Larsen spent his freshman year at little Concordia College in northern Minnesota, then went into the service. He played two years of football at El Toro Marine Base, then returned to Concordia for his degree. His coach, Jake Christensen, called Larsen "the strongest boy in the world."

Larsen was grass-green, even with the Vikings, because he hadn't played much with the Rams. In 1965 he was used mostly on special teams—the kickoff team, the field-goal team—because he just wasn't good enough on the pass rush. Larsen was great against the runs, but coming off the line so slowly, he didn't help put the pressure on the passer.

It was just a 50–50 year for the Vikings in 1965. They were beset by injuries to key personnel and they suffered some bad breaks. Somehow they couldn't get untangled. It was a seven won, seven lost year. The club was really better than that. And 1966 was a disaster. Minnesota won only four games, lost nine and tied one. And it was the same old story of frustration, blowing leads, running into red-hot players at the wrong time. For example:

Against Baltimore, Minnesota took on Johnny Unitas when the peerless passer had a chance to break Y. A. Tittle's career record for touchdown passes. Minnesota not only blew a 16–0 lead, but it was also the victim of three scoring flings by Johnny were last in their division in 1961, the club's maiden season, with a 3–11–0 record. The following year they climbed to sixth; the won-lost record was 2–11–1, but that season the Los Angeles Rams were so bad that they shouldn't have been permitted on a pro football field, as their 1–12–1 record showed. In 1963 the Vikings went one notch higher, ahead of the Rams and 49ers. They had achieved a promising 5–8–1 record. They were scoring more points and their opponents were scoring fewer, and that is what they pay off on when the ballgame is over.

So, in three years the Vikings had won ten, lost thirty, tied two. And all signs pointed to further improvement when Minnesota drafted a bruiser of an all-American lineman named Carl Eller, who was already a local favorite, having played brilliantly for the University of Minnesota.

Had it not been for football, this 6-foot 6-inch bundle of muscles might have been a $100-a-week laborer in his home town of Winston-Salem, North Carolina. But he did play football, and he played well, and he was a sure-shot all-American even before he went to college. At least the University of Minnesota scouts thought so, because he had easily earned high school all-American honors. How could this huge but still growing boy fail to improve?

The scouts guessed right about Eller. As a sophomore, he was part of a fine Golden Gopher team, which journeyed to the Rose Bowl in 1962 and knocked off UCLA, 21–3. Eller's heroics during his college career brought him nationwide attention. In a game against the University of Michigan for the coveted Little Brown Jug, the Gophers were forced to punt. Eller was the first man downfield, and he hit the receiver so hard that the ball bounced loose. Minnesota recovered and went to a touchdown, the only one scored in the game. Against Wisconsin, Minnesota found itself pushed back to its own 1-yard line. The Badgers had possession, first and goal. But they didn't crack in, because Carl Eller personally barred the door. Eller gether. Shoving people around in the Southwest Conference was far easier than blocking the big guys in the pros. Somehow, all of a sudden, he just wasn't comfortable, and he didn't know why.

The Rams gave up on Dickson quickly and traded him to Dallas. The Cowboys didn't think much of him either and dumped him on the Cleveland Browns. The Browns were swiftly disenchanted, and Dickson went to the Vikings. So, two years and four teams later, Paul Dickson tried all over again to make good in pro football.

He was less than spectacular with Minnesota, and wasn't a sure-shot regular by any means. Then somebody got the idea that a player who stood 6 feet 5 inches tall and weighed 265 pounds might do better as a defensive lineman. And that was where he found his true niche. Marion Campbell, the Viking defensive line coach, took him in hand and showed him the moves. Intelligent, thoughtful, Dickson caught on quickly. He had the natural quickness needed by a defensive lineman, and his keen, mathematical brain read the offense pretty accurately. He continued to make mistakes, naturally. Most of the time he elected to gamble, to make the big play; it didn't always work out. But Dickson was also willing to work hard, to study ways of improving his play. And he began to make great progress.

During their first few years of play, the Viking defense was awful. At one time or another, it was last in almost all departments: most first downs allowed by rushing, most touchdowns allowed by rushing, most first downs allowed in a season, most total yardage allowed in a season. Yet the front four was really better than the statistics showed, especially taking into consideration that three-fourths of the defensive line consisted of Cleveland castoffs (Jim Prestel came to the Vikings from the Browns, just like Marshall and Dickson).

The way the team climbed in the standings those first three years was an indication that better things were in store. They